SECRETS & LIES

MY JOURNEY TO ENLIGHTENMENT

BY MARK PHILLIPS

WADENA HOUSE
BOOKS

WADENA HOUSE BOOKS
PO Box PMB 326
445 East Cheyenne Mountain Blvd.
Colorado Springs, CO 80906

Published 1999 by WADENA HOUSE BOOKS

Printed in the U.S.A by Millennia Graphics
Cover Design: AXIO Graphics
Cover Photo: Ryan Cooley at Studio 2
Author Photo: Wendy Nelson at Blue Fox Studios

Library of Congress Cataloging-in-Publication Data
Phillips, Mark A.
     Secrets and Lies, My Journey to Enlightenment
     by Mark Phillips

ISBN   0-9674433-7-7

SECRETS & LIES

MY JOURNEY TO ENLIGHTENMENT

Contents

Acknowledgments

Thanks to Bob C. for making this possible.

Thanks to Bob D. for a great launch.

I have many to whom I am indebted for efforts involved in bringing this story to life in word and page. Some were there along the journey with its dangers and pitfalls. My family, Donna and her family, friends, fellow sojourners, and coworkers who were steadfast as I searched the highest and deepest realms for spiritual truth, are all a part of the ultimate victory. John, Carol, Chris, and Bryce were especially supportive during the 'cold, gray, lifeless time.' My parents and sisters were always supportive and patient, even when the quest appeared all consuming, which I guess it was.

Many helpful comments from friends and family members are manifest upon these pages. Surely all of these fine people know how appreciated they are. Thanks to my more visible friends whose courage and public support are testimony to their lives of service. Special gratitude to RC for the title help. Angela and I have enjoyed our partial living at AXIO. My three children well tolerated days when Daddy was unavailable during the writing and production of this work. How fine their learning that play time was always near.

Finally, my precious angel is the most wonderful wife within the realm of possibility. Her nurture, support, and needed urgings are forever a part of this project. As I have written before, that such love can be shown by a woman is testimony enough that there is a great and loving God, since she is one of the more wonderful creations.

It is to her that this book is dedicated.

Fellow Neophytes and Masters

Steve Martin entered my dressing room backstage at the Tonight Show. I suppose it was one of those surreal moments in life. You know, the presence of stardom and all that stuff. I had been on stage with him once before, at the Comedy Store on Sunset Strip, when I had won the National SMLAAASAC. That's the National Steve Martin Look Alike, Act Alike, Sound Alike Contest. Yet, this time was different. I was appearing on the Tonight Show with its millions of national viewers. Actually working with Steve Martin, the biggest comedy icon of the time.

But I remember thinking what a nice guy he was, and how easy this seemed in contrast with my ongoing supernatural encounters. This comedy appearance was just fantasy. My psychic endeavors were anything but phantasm or daydream. Indeed, they were very real, in both their hellish and heavenly ways.

Steve and I did not take long to work out our routine for the show later on. Then he kindly

signed my copy of his book, *Cruel Shoes*. He wrote:
"Dear Mark, Thanks for all your help
on the Tonight Show."

I took the book back from him and said,
"No, thank-*you*, Steve." Then I smirked at him
and said, "And you're welcome for all my help. I
know you couldn't have made it this far without
me."

"That's good, Mark. Self-effacing sarcasm
works well in comedy."

After I chuckled, I held open the book to
him and queried, "What's the deal with this?" It
was open to his little essay entitled 'My Uncle's
Metaphysics.' "Is this meant to be serious or
funny?" I asked.

"Mmm. A little of both I guess."

As a serious student of the disciplines of
wisdom, I was curious about such matters, so I
pushed a bit. "Steve, do you consider yourself a
student of metaphysics and mysticism?"

He replied as he got up and headed for the
door, "I suppose we all do to some extent, huh?" I
smiled and nodded in agreement. "Mark, someone will come get you when it's time to go on. Or
you can wait in the green room. Either way, I'll
see you behind the curtain then."

"Okay, Steve. Thanks."

"Sure." He smiled and quietly shut the door

as he went back to his own room.

I had no idea that two decades later, by the calendar's turning into the new millennium, experiences like the ones I share in this book would be dominating our culture. The topics of self-search and divine truth are now before us daily, and range from arts and media even into the sciences. I knew in that dressing room I was at the tip of the iceberg of the planet's convergence toward its new stage of life; but, I could not have envisioned the depth it would reach into society's very fabric by the time the early years of the new millennium would really be upon us. I would have felt so much joy in knowing where we would all be by the time I had children of my own. Today, things have grown immensely toward a greater acceptance and practice of the different disciplines which were considered on the fringe of society when I walked onto the stage at the Tonight Show.

From her CD 'Ray of Light,' Madonna sings in 'Sky Fits Heaven',, "I think I'll follow my heart, That's a good place to start." Depak Chopra advertises his *Center for Well Being* with such programs as the Healing Heart and Panchakarma. Dr. Andrew Weil's *Self Healing* newsletter draws on cultures as diverse as Harvard Medical School and the Himalayas, including a 'focus on interactive guided imagery therapy.' Larry King hosts a variety of mediums who communicate comforting messages about dead loved ones. Now, anyone can see WISDOM television, radio, and Internet focusing on spirituality and global community, delivering interviews with Wayne Dyer, Kenny Loggins, Gary Zukav, James Redfield and others. The majority of Hollywood films has at least one scene airing the notable message supervened as hope for so long: "Follow your heart. Follow your heart to know that your dreams can become your own divine realities of purity and love." Yet, there is still so much cruelty, hatred, bigotry, and soul sickness.

In nearly every city, there are almost annual fairs about crystals, magical arts, mythical dreams, pagan rituals, aura diagnosis, psychic cures, and inner-healing for divine peace. We are seeking answers as human souls turn to yoga for health and meditation for tranquillity. The Dalai Lama, believed to be the reincarnation of Avalokitesvara, is touted by many visible people as the most moral man living upon the planet. His writings grow in popularity. I recently finished his 'Essential Teachings.' Some solutions appear so simple while others still seem unknowable.

Amidst all the conventions, seminars, psychic programs and services, and books on self-mastery, society continues to accelerate in the direction to which I personally did strive with zealous fervor. We are entering a time I faintly coveted and only dreamed possible back in that dressing room at NBC-Burbank. Yet, there is still so much pain.

Long before society's current firestorm of eager desire for spiritual power, divine enlightenment, and self- comprehension, something strange happened to me. You will discover it odd indeed that through the path I took, I was finally led to a surprising and successful journey's end. As I searched for the greatest divine health, wealth, peace, and prosperity, enlightenment did become a reality. This same awareness and hope that was revealed to me is also possible for you. You will find it in these pages. May we have the wisdom to embrace it in life.

There is something I so long to say now, but prudence dictates a painful patience. In time. In time, it shall be said. It is with humble entreaty that I invite you to read to that point.

Chapter 1

Scary, Scary, Night

It was Christmas Eve. My eighteenth. Though it was the season of tranquillity, it would not be a silent night or holy night for me. I was not to sleep in heavenly peace. Soon, terror would fill every fiber of my being; but, through the months and years that followed, I would overcome the instinctive fear I felt that early morning hour that spawned my quest. I would conquer the uneasy feeling that arose within me during many more such encounters. I will share with you what led up to that night and the sixteen years that came after. I was about to embark on a journey to heaven into the bliss of cosmic consciousness. I would soon be following the blue light into the nirvana of enlightenment. Battles would be fought and blows exchanged. Blood would flow. At times, even death would ensue, but the path was the obsession. The goal became the only vision. Journey with me, my dear accomplice. Light, life, and love, my friend.

There are people who fill pews of churches every Sunday who might think I had a churchless background as a child, once they read further and see the nature of my search. But, let me put that to rest right up front. Pop Moerner (my grandfather on my mother's side) was a Methodist minister, whose father was as Lutheran minister. They had moved from Germany to the United States while my grandfather was a teenager. My father was a Sunday School teacher and lay leader in the church until he was no longer physically able to do so. His recent death ensued shortly after he was no longer active in that arena. My mother participated in the choir and other activities, and was a model of church commitment my entire childhood. Though the pages of this book reveal a young man who seems to have rebelled from those roots, I am thankful to have grown up in a secure and loving environment. Such things are not to be taken for granted. The main point is that it applied to me what is often heard: 'He was brought up in the church.'

I spent the first half of my childhood in central Texas, where the stars are so thick on a clear night that our galaxy, the Milky Way, looks like a cloud covering. Before I had even learned the alphabet, I loved lying on that mattress-like carpet grass, staring up into a vast moonless sky, reflecting on one of the first carols I ever learned in Vacation Bible School: "I love you Lord Jesus, look down where I lie, and stay by my cradle 'til morning is nigh." If he was looking down on me, it must be from up there. It was an almost eerie feeling to picture this supernatural power among that vast sky ... so huge and obvious, yet hidden from my view, counting my every breath as I pondered the vision above me. There was a chilling thrill from the very notion, especially since I could talk directly with him as was being taught to me in my Christian home. No doubt that was the main reason that I thought I wanted to be an astronaut until my sophomore year in high school. Space and flight held me in fascinated awe. But there was more to it than the thrill of air and space travel. It was the mysterious nature of that endless night sky that stirred my innermost being. Those tingling moments are some of my earliest memories. In fact, I still love star-gazing, though the thoughts behind the excitement have changed a bit.

We moved to central Tennessee when I was eight. My first love had become baseball, but another favorite pastime was developed there in Nashville, obviously influenced by my earlier years of the Texas night watches. My best friend and I would lie upon his trampoline at night looking up in search of ... oh boy ... alien life! This was especially enthralling after an episode or two of 'Twilight Zone', 'Outer Limits', or 'Lost in Space'. Oh, the things we could see, and the stories we would tell. It was no longer a Lord Messiah staring down at me, but now there were superior alien life forms, who happened to be humanoid - more like me. Therefore, I was now more like the inhabitants of the heavenlies. I liked the sound of that! It made sense, and heaven seemed more accessible to me personally.

Like most kids growing up in any American city, I did my share of playing with ouija boards, and faking seances, and trading horror stories at group sleepovers. We actually called these slumber parties, which was an oxymoron. There was very little slumber involved, and that was resisted to the last effort of the final eyelid. The best things about such activities were the discussions. I would hyper-focus every brain cell on anything regarding the supernatural.

I think I enjoyed a greater love of science fiction than the average youngster, perhaps because my love for the natural sciences was enormous. I made a mess of the bathroom ceiling on more than one occasion with my various chemistry sets. I also built miniature hot-air balloons and sent them to all kinds of places in my mind, though in reality they went only a few thousand feet above the earth. (Recently, after many dormant years from such activity, my kids and I launched another one, and it still looked to me like it went past Mars.)

I remember rushing home from school every day to check out "The Big Show' on TV at 4:00pm, because they would have a good monster flick at least once a week, hopefully on a day not dedicated to baseball practice during the season. The supernatural intrigued me, and every opportunity to experience it or create an eerie environment of the presence of big, hidden, scary things was taken. I cannot say that these are the things that drew me into my search for Truth, but they certainly did not interfere with the beginning of the journey. I still have a weak spot for science fiction, though I have little to do with the gore that comes out as an excuse for modern horror these days.

My first real experience with what might be considered under the broad umbrella of post-modern Aquarian thought came at church camp. At the impressionable age of fifteen I was guided, along with my fellow campers, through a visualization-imagery session by a cool seminary student.

He began, "Lay flat on your backs. Relax and get comfortable. Good. Now tense your right leg as you inhale deeply. Now relax your leg as you slowly exhale."

We continued to proceed through all four limbs, the back, the abdomen, and all the facial muscles. This is a good relaxation technique and can provide many health benefits, but the seminary student's session did not end there. He had more in mind for us than a lesson in relaxation and self-hypnosis. When we had become as relaxed as is possible for teenagers, he continued: "Now I want you to picture yourself walking along a road that runs next to a gorgeous river, whose sound of flowing penetrates your being. The sky is a beautiful blue and there is a gentle breeze blowing on your face. Feel it and picture this setting. Allow yourself to be truly there. Hear the water flowing and the wind rustling in the trees as your face is graced by the moving air. You have no worries. No homework, no school, no parents or brothers or sisters or friends, and no problems at all. You are at total peace. That's it, now. But ...suddenly you feel a sense of panic. The wind is turning blustery. The sky is growing dark with black and swirling storm clouds. You look behind you on the road. You cannot see anything, but you know something is there and it is chasing you.

You start running down the road, and now you dare not look back, and you continue running with all of your strength. This thing you fear is getting closer but you do not turn around. You only keep running. Suddenly, you know this thing is what you fear most in life. You realize that if you stop running, this thing will stop chasing you, and you can turn to see it. So, do that now. Turn around and see it clearly. What is it? What do you see?"

I was actually out of breath from running. I was astonished that I could see clearly what had been chasing me. How surprised I was, and disturbed. This thing was me!

Needless to say, I was very troubled. I went off alone to ponder this experience the rest of the afternoon, and dared not speak of it to anyone during our evening meal. Later that night I pulled the seminary student away from the campfire to discuss our little sprint by the river.

He was the first to speak and he said, "So, Mark, how did you like our session today?"

"Well, David, that's what I wanted to talk to you about"

"I know."

"How?"

"Listen, Mark. I saw your face when we finished today. I think you had what I would call a very significant experience. I think you really have the gift of visualization."

A gift, huh? That's usually a nice word for talent, so my fifteen-year-old ego was nicely stroked, even though I did not know what he had meant. I was reluctant to ask, but I did share what I had seen. "David, I was really scared when we were running down the road …I mean, when we were imagining that we were running down the road."

David interrupted me. "Like I said, you have a great gift. In your mind, you really were running down the road. That's why you said just now, 'When we were running down the road …' You were more or less making that little picture in your mind come alive. Sort of real life."

I was getting a bit fidgety now. I just wanted to tell him what I saw. He had already anticipated that and said to me, "But you just want to tell me about this thing you saw on the road, don't you?"

"Yes, yes. Man, I don't get how you know all that." He smiled with confidence and reassurance, urging me on with his expression. I continued, "Anyway, when I stopped on the road, I turned around and …" I paused. "David, I saw myself. Man, I can't believe it. I was afraid of myself. I mean, that just doesn't really seem very cool."

"Mark, it is very cool. Very, very cool. You're how old?"

"Fifteen."

"Fifteen, huh? There are grown men, even men as old as your grandfather, who have not learned yet that they are their own worst enemy." He could tell I was puzzled. At fifteen, this was starting to get a bit heavy, even for a science fanatic and sci-fi buff. Baseball, and now girls, were still what I would choose for my attention most of the time. "Listen to me, Mark. The greatest limitation on any man's life is himself. The Bible says that we are made in the image of God. What do you think that really means?"

I had never really given that too much thought, so I simply answered, "I don't know. What?"

David answered, "It means we are made of the same stuff, that's what. You are already starting to realize that, but some part of you knows that you hold yourself back from your greatest potential. That is why you saw yourself on that road today. You are afraid of yourself more than anything else, because you know that only you can really stop you from doing great things in life. I have a gift, also. I can tell when somebody is destined to know the secrets of the universe. I have not met very many. You are one of those people."

This inner potential jazz left me a little confused, but I got the gist of what he was saying and I was beginning to feel quite stirred with our discussion. My curious nature was intrigued, even anxious, about the idea of uncovering these secrets of the universe.

David continued, "You were on the church basketball team that won the city tournament this year. I hear you're pretty good. You made All-City, right?"

I was putty in his hands now. I replied, "Yeah, and my brother coached that team."

"I know. He did a great job. Everybody in church was really proud of you guys. Is basketball your favorite sport?"

"I really think I like baseball more. I'm a little better at that, and a little short for basketball."

David gave a little chuckle. He was under six feet tall, which was obviously my destiny as well. "Yeah, I know what you mean. OK, let's take baseball. Do you have a favorite memory about any moment when you have played before?"

I answered immediately, because it is still my favorite memory from my own baseball-playing days. I can see the baseball from that game sitting on my shelf as I write this. I answered, "Sure, the day I pitched a complete game no-hit-ter and hit a grand slam homer in the same game. My mom even kept the newspaper clipping about it."

David said, "Wow, not bad. I'll bet you relive that game a lot in your memory. I mean, you must think about it every now and then."

"Yes, I guess so,"

"Mark, let me tell you something. You can go through that same relaxation deal we did today, and relive that game or just that home run as if you were actually there, and something special will be happening. You will be taking your mind into the kingdom of heaven. You can relive some of the greatest feelings and moments you have ever had, including those to come. Now consider this. Couldn't that be what heaven is all about?"

"Sounds neat, but, I don't know. It also sounds kinda weird to me. I'm not sure I understand."

"Wait a minute. I'm not explaining this very well. You know how real your experience on the road by the river felt to you today? I mean, you would not have been so bothered by what you saw if what happened didn't seem sort of real. Do you understand?"

I answered, "I think so. It was like a good movie or something, only I helped to write it."

"That's right. Exactly. I couldn't have said it any better. My point is that you can make your own movie out of your own life." He tapped one finger on top of my head. "You can start writing the script right there in your own mind. You are created in the image of God, with the same ability to create your own life experiences just like God created the universe." He could probably tell I wasn't totally with him. "Well, it's something for you to think about, anyway."

"Yeah, thanks."

"C'mon, Mark, let's get back to the fire."

His stuff about us being able to crate the same way God created the universe sounded like a huge jump from my present status, but this day had been better than any ghost story or night watch I had ever experienced. This was closer to being the real thing. A script come to life! David was a great psychologist, too. He stroked my pride like a violin, and used this to communicate with me very well. I left church camp that summer with a curiosity about this power inside of me and this gift to uncover the secrets of the universe.

I also found this idea a bit comforting, since I had been struggling with religion lately. As a young adult (as my dad called us in Sunday School class) who was interested in science, I had run across the theory of evolution and organic origins to the universe. Obviously, this conflicted with my understanding of the biblical picture. I was beginning to pride myself in associating with modern science, and I just knew this exclusive organic origin theory must be embraced if I was to maintain this association. The thought of being able to reveal some important answers encouraged me that I might be able to resolve this dilemma.

I stared out of the church-bus window a lot on the way home, and it was not girls or the basketball city championship or baseball that preoccupied me. There was this one girl I met at camp who ran a close second, but my primary focus was on this gift David told me that I possessed. I wondered how it could be used to uncover the secrets of the universe that dominated my pensive wanderings.

I never discussed this with my dad or my grandfather, who was the elder pastor at our church. To this day, I cannot be certain as to why. Perhaps typical of some teenagers, I probably thought they would disapprove and somehow discourage this technique that might resolve my growing problems between science and religion. At any rate, my appetite had been whetted for more, and that is just what I was going to get. Well, in a year's time, that is.

Shortly after camp, we moved back to Texas.

I was a bit disgruntled about the move at first. I had become a city boy in Nashville, and the thought of moving to the small central Texas town where I had spent my first eight years was not so appealing to a high school sophomore. That soon ended. It was a great place to finish growing up, and the night sky was marvelous as ever. I reflected back on my camp experience during the next year, occasionally taking myself through the relaxation exercises. Oddly enough, I was taken through a similar mind-drama at a church camp again, but it was not as intense this time. My interest waned a little bit, but it would return during my junior year.

I was once again encouraged along this path by a nurse who had become a vocational instructor. She was directing a course connected with my hospital work program. In our high school gymnasium, she taught our class relaxation techniques very similar to those in camp. She informed us these methods came from the teachings of Buddha. She further instructed us on how to get in touch with our higher selves. We were told we could be more successful in our chosen vocations if we could tap into this perfect inner-self. Power! Success! That was for me. I began regularly practicing the relaxation techniques throughout that year, the following summer, and into my senior year.

The instructor was a lovely, attentive and

caring woman who had only our best interests in her heart. During the exercises, she regularly checked our limbs by picking them up and dropping them to see how relaxed we were. On one such occasion during the late autumn of my senior year, she commented to me that I was particularly stiff.

She said, "Mark, you have always been quite capable of turning off the world and entering a relaxed state. You are stiff today. I would ask you what is on your mind, but I think I already know."

She did know. My inability to relax that day was no doubt a reflection of the infamous 'dress-code battle', which would help shape my view of authority. The year was 1971. As student-body president, and as a student who wanted to wear his hair longer in accordance with the growing fashion of the day, I was engaging the school board in dialogue to allow greater student freedoms in this area. There were other student council officers involved in this as well. That very day, I had received an anonymous note on my car as a death threat for my activities and hearings before the school board. This seemed a pretty good reason to be a bit uptight during our meditations.

It was a small, conservative, one-high-school town that perhaps considered the changing fashions some sort of threat. Oddly enough, however, little did I know at the time, but my appeal for the families, and not the school board, to decide upon an individual's hair and attire, was actually a classical conservative position. Technically speaking, it was a position that was against undue government interference in family affairs in non-injurious matters, but I had not put all that political philosophy together. I just saw a need for a change.

And change was in the air in those days, and it was the liberals who were talking about that change, not the conservatives. All I knew was that something was wrong with the status quo, symbolized to me by this out-moded dress code. I wanted things to be different, so I ended up associating with those who were preaching for things to be different. My girlfriend was in the same camp with me. She was another Student Council officer and we talked of the big movements of improvements that our generation would bring to the world.

More important than these political associations, however, was the effect this whole dress-code affair had on my view of authority. I did not know what a personal world view was at the time, nor had I ever heard the term, but mine was being shaken. For the first time, I was thinking seriously and deeply about the fact that those in local power are not necessarily right. I knew this was true of Communist countries, but I had not applied that same reality to small-town America, where football was king, everybody knew each other, and help was just around the corner for anyone in need. There were not supposed to be closed-minded leaders with misguided fears in my home town. This was a difficult revelation for me. It was one that fueled the newly birthed desire to go within myself to find answers to some of life's tougher questions.

It also fitted the mood of the era. There was an atmosphere of newness in the air, a desire for radical alterations in the fabric of our society. Americans had grown tired of the Vietnam struggle and wanted it to end. Even the war hawks in my town were weary with the lack of resolve. I remember hearing some of the adults discussing it. "Nonsense," some would say. "Send those boys over there to win or don't send them at all." That conflict became a symbol of all that was big and ugly and wrong and out-dated.

There was an intoxication captivating my generation with the spirit of peace and love - what could be wrong with that? Even at this point in my life, I believe that much of the analysis of what was wrong with materialistic attitudes to our world, according to the 'hippie' culture, was actually correct. The problem was in our solutions. Existing institutions missed a golden opportunity at that time, and I was only one of many that was missed. (Our brave American veterans of that war were also by-passed, mistreated, and became social casualties as a result. Only much later did they start receiving some of the decent recognition which they so deserve. Perhaps it will never be enough.)

I saw the advocates of change as being right about the war and its dirty profits. This was strengthened when a friend of my older sister returned from 'Nam' with his chest, arms and hands so shot up that his promising career as a guitarist had been shattered along with his flesh and bones. My eyes filled with tears as Richard told the story of when he and his best buddy over there from New York got shot up so badly. His buddy called him 'Tennessee' and Richard called him 'the black Yank'. Richard said he heard the screaming whistle of the bullets go past his head as he hit the ground. When he looked up, his friend was face down. Richard crawled to him and turned him over and saw the massive chest wounds. His friend looked up, smiled, and said, "Tennessee, I could count my last breaths on one hand if I could feel my fingers. Peace, brother." Then he died. Richard did not want to accept this and looked up for a medic screaming for help. Then he heard the sinister whistle of the bullets again. This time he felt his chest on fire, and he hit the ground hard. He woke up on a transport to a MASH Unit.

I was so torn up about this senseless end of his brilliant music career. He was a great musician and poet, and had no business getting torn apart in a foreign jungle. I was young and confused and could not understand this. How could people in authority make decisions to allow such a thing to happen?

I also saw the new voices as being right about freedoms of expression against repressive dress codes. Philosophies were spreading that such repression reflects a deep-seated grip on our culture by the opponents of change and improvement. I absolutely loved the music coming down, and found it as captivating as my imagery exercises. And, oh, what a powerful sensation to combine the two. I wondered if perhaps these voices of change were right about morality and spiritual matters as well They were talking of new religion, new philosophy, new freedoms, and new paths to a golden age coming upon this planet.

Indeed, we were involved in the dawning of the Age of Aquarius, as we were so encouraged to be in the musical *Hair*. I was listening and learning, and eager to participate with the rest of my generation in the ground-breaking activity that would see full blossom by the turn of the century. By my eighteenth Christmas Eve, I was primed for a special Christmas visitor.

As an industrious high school senior and as part of my vocational education, I had a job in patient care at the local hospital. This was appropriate, since I was planning on becoming a physician. I worked three hours before school on three or four days a week, and three weekends a month. I was scheduled to work throughout the Christmas holidays, and chose to stay home on my own while the rest of the family went to visit relatives for a week. After all, I was old enough to take care of myself, and certainly feeling confident about life in general. From my personal growth to my great hopes for the planet due to the revolution of my generation, I just knew a great era was dawning.

Tomorrow would be Christmas Day, and I had to be at the hospital early. Knowing I had to get up at 5am, I wanted to be asleep by 11pm that night. I knew that I wanted to make Christmas a little brighter for those unfortunate people who had to be in the hospital on Christmas Day. Of course, so did I. As I drifted off, I thought a bit about Jesus, as he had always been my family's focus of Christmas ever since I could remember. I recalled the childlike anticipation of all those earlier Christmas mornings, and how I loved our church's candle-lighting service, and how the sweet melodies of carols always warmed me with a simple joy; but now I needed to enter the next stage of my life with the power and knowledge which would equip me, along with an entire generation, for personal and planetary success. Santa Claus, the Easter Bunny and the Tooth Fairy were no longer real. Neither was the Jesus of my childhood. Mixed emotions were my last feelings of the day as I drifted off to sleep before my first Christmas alone. But I was not be alone for long.

At 3am I heard an explosion in my head, and awoke with a start. I was immediately aware of a presence. It was awesome and powerful and not the least bit comforting. Dread gripped my heart. I was literally motionless with fear. In my peripheral vision (I was staring straight up), I saw a faint outline of a dark figure standing at the doorway to my bedroom. It approached my bed. It moved slowly, deliberately, and appeared to float across the room with an ethereal grace. This creature, this figure, then stood to the side of my bed and behind my head. I could feel sweat breaking out on my hairline, but I dared not move. I hoped against all odds that this was a dream, but I knew I was wide awake. Then, I felt a hand touch my forehead. "You shall know all." Did I hear that in my mind only or also with my ears? Again, "You shall know all." I did hear it! What did that mean? I must ask. I must. I mustered up all of my courage to address the visitor, but as I forced my mouth open to speak ...

The presence and my inability to move left as suddenly as they had arrived. I lay there breathing a sigh of relief that I was alone again. My fox terrier was growling at the foot of the bed. I started laughing because it was just too much like a Hollywood scene. I think my laughter also provided an emotional relief. But I thought, "This is worse than any cheap movie. This is really not very funny at all."

I was up for the day. No way I was going to sleep again the rest of that morning. In fact, I had a friend come over the rest of the week, so that I would not be on my own to face the possibility of another uninvited guest from another world. Fortunately, this distraction did not cause me to kill anybody during patient care at the hospital later that morning.

During the following months and years, my first instincts - that I had encountered something which wanted to bring me harm - were overtaken by my curiosity about the phrase 'You shall know all'. I was going to be taught that it was not evil that I had encountered that night, just raw power, the power of an ascended master. And I could learn to harness that power for myself, and use it to benefit others.

'You shall know all'. Who should I tell about this? I could just see myself trying to discuss it with the school counselor, the lady who told me to study Reader's Digest to prepare for the SAT and ACT. Furthermore, there were certainly those in town who would have liked for something weird like this to ruin my integrity during the dress-code battle. I only discussed the events of that night with my girlfriend and a few friends I could trust. I received some blank stares and also some interesting comments:

"Look, everybody has weird dreams every now and then. Don't worry about it."

"Maybe it's alien life contacting you. They sometimes come into our minds like that. I saw a special report about it on TV."

"Man, what kind of drugs are you taking anyway? That just sounds like a weird trip."

"Do you think you could be a medium? Perhaps some souls who have died are trying to contact you. It could take some time to realize you're one who channels.

"If you're really bothered about it, go see a shrink. I wouldn't mess with it though if nothing else happens. It's just one of those things in life you can't explain. Or just a dream. Don't worry about it."

Great. Don't worry about it. My new nighttime buddy is an etheral beast from Universal Pictures, but don't worry about it.

I was unable to communicate effectively the intensity of this experience to anybody.

I was having the same luck communicating to the school board the need to lighten up on their antiquated dress-code system. Once again, my interest in the psychic world was put on the back-burner in favor of the dress-code battle, as well as the preoccupation of life felt by most college-bound high school seniors. My focus was in the direction of medicine, not the search for a universal truth, or an ultimate realization that there is no such thing. I had goals I had to achieve in this world. Nonetheless, I was still plagued by earlier questions about science and religion and my inability to reconcile the two. I did want 'to know all' about that dilemma.

These concerns would carry over into my freshman year at the University, but the first semester was spent overcoming the shock of the change in academic challenge between high school and the competitive world of pre-medicine. I was also chosen as the youngest alternate delegate to the Democratic Convention and was active in the hopeless McGovern campaign. As I mentioned, I thought political liberalism was correct because talk of change was heard there, and that seemed to be what was needed. Further into the back of my mind went other philosophical concerns about life. More and more I began to focus on the natural sciences and my vision of medical school. That would be interrupted in the second semester, however. A new tractor-beam would draw me toward another world in the spring of 1973.

I took one of my two required religion courses as part of the core requirement for my liberal arts science degree. It would change my life, which I guess is one of the purported reasons for engaging in higher education. It was a course on modern Christianity and the theme of hope. We read many authors, but I was captivated by Teilhard de Chardin, a scientist-philosopher. His description of the noosphere as a single planetary consciousness was incredibly exciting. A short explanation could be to view the earth as a single living being, its mind being the noosphere. The consciousness of each person blends into this single planetary 'oversoul'. This pantheistic oneness has much akin to Buddhism. Also important to me, however, was the consideration of how physical evolution reflects a sort of spiritual evolution of the entire planet. As above, so below. This is what excited me most about the readings in the course.

What these authors were proposing seemed to bridge the gap for me between religion and science. Just as modern creatures had genetically evolved from less complex forms into more advanced beings, so was the soul of man evolving on the spiritual level into a more highly evolved species if god-man. Finally! This was the perfect marriage between science and religion. For several years I had wrestled with this dilemma, and now it seemed close to a resolution. I remember staying up with friends one night to study for a vertebrate zoology test, but we mostly discussed the noosphere and how physical evolution reflects the spiritual evolution of the planet. The prophecy of that seminary student a few years earlier seemed to be manifesting as an intellectual reality for me.

Music had become a vehicle for further revelation. This would assault any stronghold that agnosticism held on me. I was lying in my room at college, eyes closed, listening to 'Stairway to Heaven' by Led Zeppelin one afternoon. This had become a favorite pastime, enjoyed at least once a week. This song is perhaps the most classical example of the best in rock music. It has every ingredient with a head, body, and tail in a chiastic musical structure. The vocals are stirring, ranging from soft eloquence to driving rhythms which brilliantly lead into melody, overlapped with a harmonious, yet stinging guitar lead. The drums are hard-driving or totally absent where appropriate. Not a lick is missed by the bass. Perhaps it is the perfect rock song. Anyone struggling with understanding the potential appeal of rock 'n' roll would do well by an academic study of this piece. Its addictive qualities are admittedly disconcerting. The genius of such music, judged good or bad, provided a profoundly determining illumination for me that afternoon.

As the song was reaching the home stretch where the lyrics spoke to me of an inner strength - "To be a rock and not to roll" - my mind and heart were blasted with one of those obvious truths about life. I could almost hear myself thinking … and feeling, "These passions stirring within me could not come from flesh and bone alone. How could the simple survival of the species have anything to do with the emotions of compassion and empathy? How could the power of this music affect only my brain if I was here by mere accident? Hope and despair for the future must be more than biochemical reactions from that substance within my skull. I know I have just touched that intangible part of me! The spirit of life is more than just a body. The source of the effects that this music is having on me is to be found in another world besides this one that I can see and touch. This much is a certainty." I was ecstatic. I knew there was more to life than the simple material world of the atheists and agnostics. I knew they had to work very hard to embrace the absence of what is obvious.

By the end of my freshman year, I felt a joy I had not tasted for quite some time. This was due to my hopes that I could bring religion back into my life without abandoning science, both of which I dearly loved. My problem was that I could not find my own personal place in this scheme. The planet might be evolving, but I would be dead and gone in less than a century. Where did that leave me? I would start approaching an answer to that question in the summer.

I had spent so much time with the books in

my freshman year that I thought a rugged job outdoors would be a good idea. So, I got on as a steel construction worker in Nashville for the summer. I spent many hours with my two best friends. Along with having an astute mind, Stryker was a former All-State tackle with a generous heart. Ted was a Merit Scholar with a keen wit and great sense of humor. I shared what had stirred me that year and found it interesting that similar experiences had occurred with them.

The music of the group Yes was speaking to us of bright and positive New Age hopes. The instrumentation was definitely beyond this world, just like the feelings if gave us. Great emotional highs could be reached especially with encounters of the song and album 'Close to the Edge'. Our hearts would burn as a sign that the lyrics read as scriptural truth. This further supported my belief that a spirit world existed, and that we humans could find our place in it, corporately and individually. If I was indeed innately divine, then I could trust the fiery passions of what my heart determined as truth. These feelings were reinforced with an occasional supplement of illicit substances. We believed this would increase our ability to see into the spirit world. Such practices were sweeping our culture with guidance from the likes of Timothy Leary, whom I considered quite the folk hero.

One weekend, we drove down to Florida to visit Stan, Stryker's older brother. He provided more life-changing mind-expansion. He introduced me to yoga, meditation and eastern mysticism, and other self-help methods of self-enlightenment. These seemed so fresh to our culture then, yet they have now become an integral part of life for so many. As I speak to people who are currently involved in these activities for the first time, they remind me of the mesmerizing awe I felt when I was just a beginner. A mystical honeymoon.

As our occasions with Stan continued, we had some fabulous supper-to-dawn discussions. "Okay, guys, here's something for the next hour," he would say. And on and on we would go about things eternal, infinite and infinitesimal.

My two best friends and I were talking with him one night. "So, Stan, who or what is God then?" I once asked. We were enjoying a bag of potato chips at the time.

He pulled one from the bag, and held it up for all to see. "This. God is this potato chip."

I tried not to burst out laughing because I did not want to appear shallow, as if I didn't understand. Of course, I was shallow, and I didn't understand. I failed in my efforts to contain, but kept it to a strong death-defying chuckle. I then coughed and cleared my throat to speak.

"Uh, Stan. I will just have to ask you plainly how it is that God is a potato chip. You know, the one that you are now swallowing?"

Stan displayed that wonderful, gentle smile that reflected his enormous intellect. "There are several good answers to that question, Mark." (They all got a kick out of putting the word 'question' before my name when having discussions about questions of the universe - sort of a comic cosmic symbolism. Question. Mark. Get it?) Stan looked the three students over as he continued, "First, God can be what you make it to be. A sports addict considers the game on TV to be his god. A potato chip addict might consider that chip or a whole bag, or a storehouse of chips. A heroin addict considers his drug to be his god. Get the drift?"

Stryker addressed his older brother. "That sounds more like religion than God. Surely there's a difference."

Stan responded, "Very good, little brother. Quite so. That is why that explanation is not so good. But listen carefully to this. That chip is part of the universe, right?"

We all nodded in obedient agreement. Ted (Mr. Humor) poked at Stryker and shook his finger as if to urge the importance of understanding that the potato chip was part of the universe.

Stan continued, "Since it is part of the universe and we are talking about God, we must define what those two things are, that is ... God and Universe. And the simplest explanation is that they are both the same thing. God and the universe are one. Wherever God is, the universe is there. And wherever the universe is, God is there. But now we must add something very important to this. By definition, God is complete and perfect. If something is not perfect, it cannot be God. Right again?"

Obedient nods again.

"Therefore," he continued, "the universe is actually already perfect. We must bring ourselves in line with this perfection by achieving our own state of godly perfection." Stan then established that all religious leaders are trying to teach this universal truth. He concluded, "That's what the Christian Bible hints at with the Trinity. You know - Father, Son, and Holy Ghost. Separate, but all one God. Each one is considered by Christians to be totally God. And they are right, but there is more to it than that. The so-called Trinity was really just a symbolic way for Jesus to communicate that all the fragments of the universe are complete in and of themselves, but are part of this single force we call God."

We three younger ones gave a unanimous hypnotized 'Wow'. The sound was properly emu-

lated on film years later by the characters Bill
and Ted in their *Great Adventure.*

I responded with my mind full of its years
of church background. "I thought Jesus was God
incarnate."

Ted gave a mocking tough guy, "Yeah, what
about that?"

Stan said, "He was and is. But the point is
that he was trying to tell everybody that we all
could be. Each one of us. Think of some of the
things he said: 'The kingdom of heaven is within
you.' 'You are the light of the world.' He was really trying to say that we already are that magical light. We just don't realize it yet. He realized
it. That is why we can say of him that he was God
incarnate. He had perfected his human evolution."

Wham! Evolution! That hit me like a mete-
orite. I remembered the concepts of physical and
spiritual evolution from my religion class, and here
was Stan talking about the same thing. When I
brought up Teilhard de Chardin, he had not heard
of him at that time, yet he was speaking the same
language, using the same terms. To me, that was
confirmation that this must be the way things are.
This must be the truth. My heart burned with joy
and absolute acceptance of this truth.

I had learned in my first year of science
study that greater credence is often given to theo-

ries independently derived and supported by more than one science experiment at different institutions, especially if they were blind of the other's activities. Here for me was the same philosophical approach to life from different independent sources. What they were saying was that Jesus had evolved to this perfect level of god-man, and that this was possible for us all. But how could I do it?

I said, "Man, this is incredible. I am just high from all of this. But, uh ... what happens to me if I die before I get properly enlightened?

Stan answered matter-of-factly, "Simple. You just keep coming back until you get it right. Reincarnation. Some of the wiser people have been around a few more times than everybody else. They really are older and wiser. Do you think that the injustices of where, when, and how different people are born is fair? We were born in the wealthiest land of freedom where we can stay up all night discussing these kinds of things. But some poor kid is born in the middle of a famine and starves to death before he can even learn to speak. Shouldn't he have the same chance you should have? Shouldn't you have the same chance as a billionaire's son? Some are born to royalty. Some are born to inescapable poverty. All these differences can be worked out through reincarnation. You are basically learning and evolving into spiritual perfection. What lesson you miss this time around can be dealt with on your next journey through humanhood."

That night's discussion took us into another sunrise. I was floating with anticipation and didn't go to sleep until late the following night. Stan had been like an angel of light bringing the good news. Again I remembered what the seminary student had told me four years earlier - that I had a gift to uncover the secrets of the universe. I believed I had just tasted of the revelation he must have meant. Best of all, I was going to become a superior being like the ones I stalked from Ted's trampoline. I would become the perfect self-actualized man, the God just like the Jesus who watched me from the stars when I was only a babe. I knew where I was going now and it was time to figure out how to get there.

Chapter 2

Cow Patties, Mushrooms, and the Vital Force

What would possess young men to steal away into the night, sneak onto a farm in Georgia, and steal mushrooms growing on cow patties? The answer in my case is probably obvious to you by now. A search for the truth, of course. I guess the same was true for Ted and Stryker. Was there truth to be had by ingesting a fungus that grows on a cow's feces dropped on the red clay of Georgia? Well, I thought so. At least I thought it couldn't hurt.

Squeezing through the barbed-wire, we felt the southern humidity slapping us in the face. The heat never lifts during the hottest months in the deep south. With flashlights perusing the field amidst the sleeping cows, we watched for farmers with shotguns, bulls with horns, and the paydirt of the mushrooms. This was just another sampling

51

of the psychic summer when my soul was being awakened to cosmic truths. I had to figure out how to evolve to the higher self. If the psilocybin from the mushrooms could help, then so be it. Of course, this might paint a rather disgusting picture of strangely enticing danger. Nonetheless, I would pay any price for enlightenment.

As it turned out, such devices were nothing more than door openers as far as mystical enlightenment goes. The best they could do was to substantiate the existence of another realm. So many of the youths at that time wanted to use these substances to party. But I was above all that. I wanted enlightenment. Right?

Oh, man. Who was I kidding? How ignorant and pompous! Still, there was one psil-induced experience with Stan that allowed me to understand that I was indeed able to separate my consciousness from my body. It scared me though. I could feel myself floating above the car as we drove along the Florida beach, but it was unsettling. I preferred the greater control I felt I had in yoga and meditation. However, this occasion in July helped to round off my psychic summer. I drove back to Nashville believing I had achieved a greater understanding of my world and my destiny. I finished out my summer job as a steel construction worker. In August, I drove back home to central Texas. I thought school would be rather dull after all of this. I was wrong.

Baby, you ain't seen nuthin' yet. I had no idea how much that statement would apply to my occult endeavors by the time I started my sophomore year in college. I was going to learn that I had personally encountered an ascended master on Christmas nearly two years earlier. Though I was learning to relax and meditate, I had no idea where that was about to take me. Though I had begun yoga, I did not yet fully understand the extent of discipline and mastery in which I would engage. Though I had dabbled in karate the previous year, I did not know I would soon experience the art of spirit defense. Though I had tasted the power of music in my soul, I had not fully come to appreciate how I could become one with the sound. As a matter of fact, I would soon start learning to become one with the wind, the sun, the moon, the stars. Indeed, at-one-ment with the universe, with life, and with Truth was on my near horizon. There was one thing I knew for sure as we all returned to school. I had an insatiable appetite for things eternal. I had to know the ultimate truth of the universe, and was willing to give up all I had for that priceless pearl. I believed I had the gift to unlock these secrets, and I wanted to cash in my gift certificate for the prize.

In reading the works of Ouspensky, Ferguson, Bailey, and eastern mystics, I was certainly beginning to question how much random chance played in our personal lives. From my college work, I knew the electron orbiting around the nucleus of an atom was theoretically everywhere in its orbit all at once; but I also knew we couldn't determine its location and measure its momentum at the same time. This 'uncertainty principle' was a nice summarizing symbol which revealed the limits of science. Furthermore, the atomic models and electron definitions were functional theories, not absolute realities. I had learned a lot about how biological systems work; but I also knew there were many things we could not measure. My East Indian biology and physiology professor referred to those things that cannot be measured as the vital force. I knew that appearances often tricked us into thinking we aimlessly drifted from one circumstance to another or the exact opposite, that we had full control of our lives and our destiny. I was learning that in actuality it is neither random chance nor our own full control that dictates our lives. There is a subtle force, perhaps tied into the vital force, that gently sways us to and fro amidst our needs to learn our lessons toward perfection, to nirvana, to a time when we could be personally capable of exercising full control.

I was beginning to learn that all the hurts and disappointments in life serve a great purpose of training each of us to reach new levels of universal mastery. I could somehow find answers to the questions that plagued me: "Seek and ye shall find." There were secrets to be discovered: "Knock and the doors shall be opened." The riches of the universe were available to him who conquered. We each had available to us comfort, hope, joy, understanding, health, wealth, peace, and prosperity: "Ask and it shall be given." All the trials and blessings of life were working together to shape each person into a cosmic master through as many lifetimes as it would take. Therefore, I did not consider it an accident when I hooked up with my old friend Olan.

I had known Olan since kindergarten. He was the perfect definition of the typical genius. He was socially awkward, but strangely likable with a good nature and generous heart. He would drop whatever he was doing to help anyone. He had enormous mental energy and most people would become exhausted from his erratic presence within less than half an hour, and back away nodding their heads as if to still be listening as he was still speaking. I have always enjoyed my time with this fascinating creation known as Olan. (He recently paid a visit in Oxford, and his intellect was as spellbinding as ever).

University registration was the week before Labor Day Weekend, 1973. It was a typical windy and sunny late summer day in central Texas. I saw him at the Student Union Building and yelled across the library lawn, "Hey Olan, where have you been?" I jogged over to see what he had been up to.

"Mark, you're the one who's been in Nashville all summer. How was it? I've been right here in Georgetown. Kinda been a boring summer, but I built a new ruby LASER and a Kirlian photography unit. Do you want to come see? Oh wait, I think I need to finish registering for this semester's courses. Well, I have already started, but Dr. Black wasn't at the physics desk, so I thought I might get some books at the library, and go back into registration after that. But I could go home and show you some really cool stuff and then see if he's back after that. Have you had lunch yet? Listen . . . "

I interrupted, "Slow down, man. The stuff sounds great, but why don't you make sure you are registered for all your classes first." I knew he might forget if he started into something else. Definitely one of those genius ADHD types. (Actually, this is what my wife often says of me, though she usually leaves off the genius part).

But he insisted, "No, it won't take long. We'll have lunch at my house. Dr. Black will be back later."

I didn't argue. He lived right across the street from campus, about a two minute walk from where we were talking. Besides, I thought I could remind him to finish registering after lunch and escort him back to the Student Union. "Okay, let's go see what you've got."

Entering his workroom was like a journey into sci-fi heaven and a neatness-fanatic's hell. I was certainly no neatness freak, so it was always a funtime in Olan's world of science mania. He showed me the ruby LASER first. We burned a few things. It was dangerous and thrilling. But he was most excited about the Kirlian photography unit. He took a photo of my aura. He laid out several other photos of different auras including plants, a cat's paw, other people, even of some slime molds.

Naturally, I asked, "Olan, this seems really cool, but, what exactly is Kirlian photography, and what is this aura it is capturing on film?"

Olan got very serious. He was almost calm in his silence before he spoke. Now that was weird and unusual for Mr. Hyperactive. "Mark," he almost whispered. "You remember the vital force

Dr. Rajah talked about in biology and physiology?"

"Yes," I responded. It is probably needless to say, but I was very interested now.

He went on, "I am convinced the auras in these photos are this life force. And look how they change between life forms, and even between different people. I want to do some experiments with different emotions and see if the aura changes on a person, like with different kinds of music, or watching a sad movie. Things like that. It could really be a fascinating study."

"Wait a minute, Olan," I said, holding my hand up indicating a desire for a few moments of silence. I paused a bit.. My wheels were spinning in my head now! Could it be that science of this physical world could actually measure things of the spirit world? Is there some point where these two regions of reality meet, and we can actually locate and observe that point? Then I spoke up, "I thought things like that just couldn't be measured, but you're telling me, showing me, we can basically corroborate the existence of the spirit world. If this is true, I mean. . . Well, this is incredible. Unbelievable!"

"I know, Mark. It's really neat, isn't it?"

"Neat? Oh, man, it's more than that! This could be the breakthrough of the century. Of scientific history. I mean, what's the deal here? How did you discover this thing?"

"Well, it's not my discovery, " said Olan. "Actually, people have been doing this for some time now. Most scientists have laughed it off as heat or something like that. Actually, it can be manipulated through heat on inanimate objects like a rock, but that could just mean that this life force has a real heat factor to it, and it is the heat of the life force that is being picked up in the Kirlian photo."

I then asked, "Well, what does happen with inanimate objects? If they have this aura, then what's the big deal?"

Olan responded, "That's the strangest thing of all. Sometimes they might show up something, and sometimes it's blank where the aura should be. And I haven't seen that it is tied in with the temperature of the object, even relative to the temperature of the air around it. What do you think this could mean?"

I thought back to Stan's statement about God being that potato chip he was about to eat. I wondered if this aura was somehow related to this god-force of the universe. I wondered if Olan had come across any philosophy like that. That God was nothing more and nothing less than everything. I decided to fish him out on this, but I only carefully hinted at it when I said, "Perhaps this life force is not just in living creatures, but can be found in everything. Maybe it's some kind of omnipotent presence found throughout the universe. Maybe it's not always picked up in the Kirlian photo. The limitation may be our ability or inability to measure it in its different states in different objects, whether alive or not. Maybe it's like Dr. Rajah said, that belief in a vital force is not just faith, because it is also reasonable to think there is more to us than just the right combination of chemicals. And maybe this vital force is everywhere in everything. Sometimes our limited instruments can measure it. Sometimes they can't. We see that kind of thing in all branches of science. No experiment is ever perfect in its reproducibility."

I couldn't believe how much I had said. Was my old friend going to think that I was nuts. I was relieved to see Olan smile with approval at these words. Then he said, "Mark, I want you to hear something."

He pulled a Moody Blues record from its sleeve and stuck it on his fine Gerard turntable. I had always dug their music but I had never gotten into the lyrics as I had with the group 'Yes.' He handed me the lyric sheet and asked me to read along as we listened to a few songs. It was astounding. They were singing about the same belief system that I was starting to embrace. Apparently this knowledge was being proclaimed all over the planet. Something big really was going on! I asked Olan how long he had been into this stuff.

He answered with a question, "Why? Do you know what they are talking about?"

I came clean, "Yes, I do. I've been getting into this whole metaphysical scene lately. I mean, if that's what they are talking about. What do you think?"

Olan was ecstatic. He replied, "I think the same thing. This whole planet is preparing for a major shift in evolution. A lot of the music these days is talking about it."

I couldn't believe this was Olan. I was more than relieved. I said, "I just thought you sat in here building LASER toys. Since you're into this kind of thing, I wonder if you've heard of the group Yes."

"Sure, but it's a little too much hard rock for me, but their lyrics are really cool. A friend of mine is really into their music. Have you met Jay Binkshop?"

"No. Is he a student here?"

"Yes. Another physics guy, I think. I really don't know what he is studying at school, but I know he is in some organizations that actually train you in how to apply knowledge about auras and the power of thought and meditation. Stuff like that. He's coming by tomorrow night. You want to meet him?"

"Well, sure thing," I answered. "This sounds great! What groups are these?"

Olan answered, "I don't know too much about them. That's why he's coming over. To show me some of their lessons and junk. Mental mastery. Cosmic illumination. Enlightenment of higher truths. Secrets of the universe."

I joked with him, "Trivial little things like that, huh?"

Olan laughed, then looked down while taking a deep breath. He looked up at me and said, "Mark, I think I am going to join. You might want to do that too."

Olan probably had no idea how interested I was. A real organization to teach these secret powers with which I was becoming obsessed. We had lunch, and I did remember to make sure he got back to registration, where we made arrangements to meet at his house the next evening after dinner (supper as we would say in Texas).

Jay was already there when I arrived. He was a really nice guy. I thought he might be like a pompous cosmic master or something, but he was just another college student. He did have an air of secrecy and seriousness about the Ancient Mystical Order. He informed us that in some ways just about anybody could get into AMO, but that in other ways it was kind of a big deal after you joined. When I asked him to clarify, he came right out and said, "You can expect a psychic visitation shortly after obtaining membership. Some new students are aware when it happens. Some aren't. But, believe me, they will come to your room and visit."

I responded, "That sounds a bit spooky to me. I've got to tell you about something that happened to me." I proceeded to give an accurate rendition of my eighteenth Christmas morning.

Jay seemed quite pleased with this. He said the description was very authentic of a personal audience with an ascended master. The terror that I felt was normal. He went on, saying, "Think about the stories you have heard in the Bible about people coming in contact with 'angels of the Lord.' " He held his fingers up in quotation marks as he continued, "These 'angels' in the Bible are ascended cosmic masters like the one that came into your room that night. That is the reason those people like Daniel trembled at their presence. The power of their mastery makes them scary, but don't we all feel a natural attraction to that kind of thing? I mean, on the one hand, stuff like that frightens us, but on the other hand we fill movie theaters to feel that kind of supernatural fear."

Jay had nailed that one straight on the head! Change is a scary thing for all of us, even when it is change for improvement. On the one hand, self-protection makes us fear the presence of the ascended master; but, on the other hand, we are drawn to it because something inside of us tells us that we need to progress. It is natural to be drawn to this spiritual growth. We concluded that re-incarnation had led those such as us to this stage in our evolution, and that we were preparing to make big leaps into the next stage of consciousness, closer to the perfection of the ascended masters, and this is why we had this natural affinity for things like sci-fi and monster movies while we were kids. I told them about my friends back in Nashville, and we came to realize that a lot of people who enjoyed sci-fi growing up were now involved in these spiritual searches for self-mastery. It was the lure of the essence of Truth to be found behind these Hollywood supernatural thrillers that was really drawing us. It's not that everybody who enjoys sci-fi ends up studying mystical truths, but the mental energy behind both is sometimes the same, and these two worlds can often overlap with certain individuals. We were such.

I made it clear that I was ready to join AMO. He had the forms with him. We filled them out and left them with him. He said the organization would be in touch. I heard from them two weeks later. It would be during an afternoon nap.

Living in a college fraternity house is not the ideal place to develop a disciplined lifestyle for a would-be yoga master. Music, girls, recreational substances, and all kinds of abounding distractions were everywhere. I had done more than my share of partying the year before, and I was needing to move onto something else now, though I would occasionally dip into the college coiffures of fun and leisure. It was almost impossible not to do so in that environment. Though they were a great bunch of guys, most of the frat-rats who inhabited the place were not really concerned with cosmic truths at that particular time of their lives. Some of them weren't even concerned about college classroom truths. Further, my psychic endeavors were not enhanced any by the fact that I was in the pre-medical program. The time involved for this was very demanding.

Nonetheless, that is where I found myself at that juncture. When time allowed, I would lock my bedroom door in the fraternity house, turn on my fan to block out the noise, and sit in the lotus position to focus on the master within and carry forth toward self-mastery. Furthermore, I had two very close friends there who were also pre-med. They too were serious about school and life, though they also enjoyed a good sense of humor. They did not consider these endeavors to be so weird, and both ended up joining the AMO themselves. My friendship with Nick taught me patience, as that was his great gift. My friendship with Mike taught me persistence and the importance of a positive attitude, as that was his gift, though his ability to complain would usually keep me in stitches with laughter.

One afternoon, we had just finished the year's first physiology lab together. I wanted to get some yoga and meditation in before supper, so to my room and the soothing fan I went. September afternoons in central Texas can be quite hot, and our science building was not air conditioned. Consequently, I was a bit exhausted from the lab and my yoga workout, so I decided to squeeze in a short nap. I have always enjoyed them and found them to be rejuvenating, even if it's for just ten or fifteen minutes. I was meditating in the lotus position on the floor (legs double-crossed, arms extended, palms up with wrists resting on the knees, and thumb and forefinger touching). I became so sleepy that I just stretched out my legs and laid flat on my back, and started to drift off.

Whap! I had heard that sound before. An explosion in my head. I felt that uncomfortable presence but it was a bit more tolerable this time. I was able to stay calmer and take in this experience with an observing attitude, rather than as a victim of intrusion. I was not unfamiliar with the reality behind this encounter. I was staring up at the white ceiling when a black, but transparent eye appeared before my vision. The size was about two feet across. I knew it represented the presence of an ascended master. A deep voice spoke through this vision. It almost sounded like a crowd of people speaking in unison. It said, "I am your chosen teacher. I will master you through your lessons." The presence and my feeling of frightened euphoria left as suddenly as they did on that Christmas morning two years earlier. I thought to myself, "Life is really getting weird, but now I am just hungry." I headed to the student cafeteria. I had worked up quite an appetite.

At supper, I ran into Reba, a girl I had dated a few times during my freshman year. She was an agnostic then, so we had enjoyed some pretty good discussions after my religion course which had once again sparked my curiosity about the supernatural. I didn't go into detail about my specific afternoon guest but I shared a little bit about where I thought I might be headed. Surprisingly, she had started to entertain the idea that there was a spiritual world behind this physical one. She had come to accept that there probably was more to life than this three-dimensional world. I took this as more evidence that something big was unfolding on this entire planet. Something that would move the entire human race into its next stage of evolution on the spiritual hierarchy. It had touched Reba's mind in the same way it was infiltrating the entire planetary consciousness. Reba was very bright and engaging, but she had been most stubborn about her agnostic position the year before. If she could be reached, anybody could.

I looked up Jay after eating. I had to tell him about what had occurred that afternoon. Fortunately, he was in his dorm room when I went by there. I knocked upon his door. He opened. He seemed genuinely glad to see me.

"Mark, how's it going? You heard anything from AMO?"

I answered, "Well, maybe. I'll ask you what you think? Something happened this afternoon."

"Really? Like what? Oh, come on in, man."

We sat down near his built-n study desk, where we propped our feet for discussion. I explained to him my unusual nap from earlier that day.

He responded, "Well, that's it then. You have heard from the AMO."

I was a bit surprised that he seemed so sure and matter-of-fact about it. I asked, "Are you sure? I mean, how do you know it was them?"

He went over to his bookshelf while explaining that my description was a familiar one from lots of new members. He pulled out a book and tossed it up in one hand, then flipped it to me. My baseball hands made a clean catch. It was one of his copies of J. Monroe's *Journeys Out of the Body*. "You're ready to read this one, Mark. I think you are already practicing astral projection."

"Astral projection?" I asked.

"Yes. By now, you know there is more to you than just your body. Astral projection is just a term for your consciousness leaving that body. Some people call them out-of-body experiences or OOBS. That sounds like a dirty word to me," he chuckled, "so I like astral projection. Other terms for the same thing are soul travel, thought or mind travel, or mind projection, although that is more of a witchcraft term, a word description for using the power of thought to shape one's reality. Anyway, it is really your astral body that is leaving your physical body. It's like this. We are both sitting in this dorm room now, but we can get up and leave it. Pretend this dorm room is your physical body, and you sitting there could be your astral body. You can get up and walk outside of this room. The same thing applies to your mind inside your body, but you have to learn to do it in the same way a baby must learn to walk. It comes more naturally to some than to others, perhaps depending upon their needs for spiritual growth. Right now, the whole race generally knows how to physically walk and it comes pretty easily to most babies. It's different with astral projection. At present, it only comes easier to a few people. Eventually, when we are in the next stage of human evolution, it will be just another skill that comes naturally to everybody."

With some concern and confusion, I responded, "Well, if we can take our minds or astral bodies anywhere, what is to keep us from getting into someone else's body? And if I leave my body, why can't somebody else move into mine while I am visiting outer space or wherever? It sounds like there could be lots of problems as more and more people develop this skill."

Jay laughed, but not meaning to make me feel stupid. He said, "Sorry. I'm only laughing because I thought the same thing when I first heard about this. I guess it's only natural. Here's the deal. Each person has what is called a silver cord or life cord attaching the astral body to the physical. This is the connector of mind and body, and it cannot be broken. It is severed upon death, but it cannot be the cause of someone dying. Nobody can break your life cord. If you are on an astral trip and decide to go home, you can just relax and you will always fall right back into your body because of the cord. It is the connection of the vital life force."

I was relieved. "So, nobody can force me out of my own body."

He answered, "That's right." The he paused and looked pensive before speaking again. He was obviously choosing his words more carefully as he said, "Now, I don't want to frighten you, but there are some mischievous entities out there, who sometimes play a little rough. What I mean is they may try to scare some travelers into thinking they will break their cord and take over their body. I think Jesus encountered some of these delinquents in the biblical possession stories about demons. Probably what really happened was that these possessed people had developed their astral skills a bit quickly and got into areas where they did not belong. The so-called demons were more highly skilled travelers who wanted to teach them a lesson, and convinced the victims that they had become possessed by giving up their physical bodies. Jesus came along and told the fear-mongers to get lost and set the victim straight about the fact that nobody can take over his body. He most likely accomplished this on some kind of spiritual plane that was not apparent to those standing around witnessing the release of the possessed person. There are not entities out there who can forcibly take over your body even if they try to convince you that they can.'

"Besides, Mark, as a member of the AMO, you won't have to worry about anything like that. The ascended masters of the organization will be constantly guarding over you from any cosmic bullies. This is where the term guardian angel came from. Besides, no one can really develop psychic skills to any great degree, unless they have good intentions. These so-called demons of the Bible were really just entities on their way to mastery who had not fully released their personal egos yet. Since they were still rather egotistical about their new skills, they were showing off a bit by acting like the cosmic playground bullies. But they could never get to the level of an ascended master behaving the way they apparently did in the Bible. There is nothing to fear from them."

We talked a bit further about the 'fear-factor' as I was starting to call it. I knew those feelings were just because I was in the presence of power, but I hated that uncomfortable queasiness nonetheless. He assured me that the fear associated with these encounters would lessen with time and experience, and would eventually disappear as I developed my own psychic skills. As I was leaving, he reminded me that I would hear from the AMO by mail soon, and would probably have my first lessons with the introductory packet.

Sure enough, I received my official acceptance letter from the AMO the next day. And included were my introductory packet and my first lessons.

Back in my room at the fraternity house, I tore open the manila envelope containing the teachings that would help set me on my path to freedom and enlightenment. I was anxious to get started. Included were instructions on how to set up a study sanctum, a sort of alter to the light of truth. I used my desk for this since it was already set up for study. It was to face the east, respectful symbolism of the ancient eastern mystery schools, especially those of Egypt and India. The two candles placed on either side represented the illuminating knowledge that would soon be imparted to me. A mirror was to be placed upon the wall where I would be studying my lessons. I wasn't sure of the purpose for that at this point, but it had something to do with self-reflective study for personal growth. It was further recommended that a linen or cloth be placed upon the desk as a sort of holy cloth, to represent the fact that this place of learning was to be a sanctuary from the rest of the world during the lessons.

It should be kept in mind that this was set up in my room at the fraternity house, so this whole arrangement was only temporarily put in position during each session. As soon as it ended, the mirror was taken off the wall, the candles, and linen cloth were removed. The desk once again looked like it belonged to a college student as I put my biology and chemistry books on it, along with some baseball magazines. There were some really ugly uniforms in the major leagues at that time, although they got even worse during the disco era. I can recall laughing at the contrast between my sanctum covering and those hilarious outfits glaring off the covers. All this was done before I unlocked my door. At that time, I was not feeling particularly evangelistic about the AMO or anything spiritual for that matter, especially in this setting. I just wanted to study, learn, apply, and progress toward spiritual perfection into godhood.. I did not want to defend my curiosity about these matters to my fraternity brothers. Nor did I want to answer questions. I wanted to ask them. I could teach after achieving some self-mastery.

Along with my weekly lessons, I read Monroe's *Journeys Out of the Body* several times during the next few months. I also began to experience the regal freedom of mind-flight. I was astral projecting quite frequently. Sometimes it would be a journey around campus. Others would include light years to distant stars and novas. Most would be alone, but there were occasions where I would be accompanied. I must admit that there were times when my astral companions were less than normal or comforting in the way they appeared. Often, I would have the feeling of being watched, even manipulated, and the setting would be one of dark clouds and mist as might be conjured up by likes of Salvador Dali.

There were two regulars who frequented my travels those first few months. One was a very slender dark 'man' about nine feet tall. If he was a physical being, he would most likely weigh about 100 pounds. The only communication I ever got from him was that his name was Ur. The other was a more fair-skinned and stockier guy. He had a bald head and made me think of a genie, which is what I called him. The unusual thing about him was the giant ruby in his forehead.

On one occasion, Genie mentally communicated to me to focus on the ruby. I had been meditating in my bedroom at home one weekend while I was there doing laundry. (This was most convenient because my parents' house was just minutes from the campus, and Mom was often glad to help, something to which I am sure most moms can relate!) As I awoke with the familiar startle and ear blast, I immediately sat up and saw Genie poking his body through my outdoor bedroom wall. I fought to ignore the fear and chills. A message came to my mind, "Focus on the ruby and project your astral body through it. Use it as a doorway." Whoosh! I found myself in a translucent red tunnel for about two seconds and then I was standing on my front lawn.

I had a euphoric feeling of boundless energy and soared into the air about 500 feet with a single leap. How amazed I was to see my father's car turning from University Avenue onto Hutto Road. I watched as it made the final turn into16th street on the way to our driveway. "Could this be?" I thought with great anticipation. I closed my eyes and let myself fall, which I had discovered would take me straight back to my body. Indeed, with a deep gasping inhalation, I woke up on the waterbed where this had all started. I pulled myself together, and got up.

Imagine my amazement as I went into the garage just as my father was pulling into the driveway. He was a vice-president of my university at the time, and my vision had witnessed him heading home from that direction. I greeted him, "Hi, Dad. Did you have to work today?"

"Yes. I just had a few things to tend to at the office. What brings you home today? Could it be laundry?"

"Yes, sir." I wanted to ask which way he had come home without revealing why I wanted to know. I mean, I could just hear myself telling him I wanted to validate whether or not I was projecting my astral consciousness out of my body above our house. He might want to send me straight into a drug rehab facility or something. I continued, "I saw some work being done on University Avenue earlier near Hutto. Is that still going on?"

He answered, "Mmm. Don't know. I went to town before and after the office today. I went on 15th Street both ways. Why?"

So, he had not come home by way of University Avenue. Again, I did not really want to tell him that I was trying to empirically validate an astral experience. It wasn't pleasant to keep things from people, especially family, but the spirit of these endeavors had such a secretive air. I assumed it was because this was knowledge that was not necessarily meant for everyone, as the AMO was teaching. These secrets amounted to powerful psychic tools into which only those ready should be initiated. I answered, "Oh, I was just curious. They don't seem to do much road work in Georgetown. I guess there's not enough traffic and bad weather to stress the roads."

"That's it exactly. Where's your mom?"

"She's in the sewing room."

"Good. You going to be around for supper?"

"Yes, sir."

"Great. See you in a bit." He headed for the back of the house where Mom was.

"Okay, Dad."

I was hopeful but also disappointed and a bit confused about the information. I was excited that I had actually witnessed my dad driving home, but I saw him turn onto Hutto from University Avenue, not from 15th Street, the parallel street one block away. Why was that? In some ways, this was definite confirmation that I had just been at the ethereal crow's nest 500 feet above my house. However, what I saw was not exactly accurate. I saw my dad coming home as he was actually coming home; but, I had one of the roads wrong. This was really strange. I could not explain it.

I had another similar experience in the fraternity house two weeks later. During one of my afternoon nap/meditations, I sat up with the blast in my head that was becoming protocol now. I struggled to completely free myself from my body and stand in the middle of my bedroom, facing the locked door, with my back to where I had been lying. Suddenly it dawned on me that if I was out of my body, I could turn and see it on the floor where I had left it. As I slowly began to turn around and look down, I became frightened at what I might see. If I was really lying there, wouldn't that be a little creepy? Of course it would, but I had to know. My curious nature has always been a blessing/curse combination, and this circumstance was no exception. Slowly I turned my ghostly head and directed my eyes to the floor. Indeed, there my body was, with mouth hanging open and tongue half out as if dead. The color was a sickening olive, and it could have been another entity taking hold of that body that was supposed to be mine. It was a horrifying image and I drew a deep breath of startled disbelief, and felt myself sucked back and awoke sitting up, taking my physical hands and checking over my physical body to see if all was still well. For a few brief seconds, there was confusion between the two bodies, because the inner feeling of controlling the movements in my physical body felt the same as it had just felt in my astral body.

This was getting to be a bit much, but I had become overly enthralled with the utter ecstasy of absolute freedom sensed during these projection experiences. Though I was a bit disturbed,

I wanted to continue, especially since I still had 'the feeling.' This is how I had come to name a sort of drowsy state combined with a knowing expectation that if I could relax and sleep, I would awaken to an astral experience. I have always had the ability to cat-nap. I can lie down and be asleep in 30 seconds for 15-30 minutes of rejuvenating afternoon rest. 'The feeling' at that time was like this, plus the almost self-fulfilling prophecy of astral expectation.

I stretched back out on the floor, and added a blanket. I noticed that my body temperature often went very low during these times, and I would sometimes come out of it very cold. This is most unusual, as I am normally hot-natured, especially when sleeping. Sure enough, I was out in less than a minute, and struggled to free myself from my body again. I did not look back this time. Instead, I thought I would experiment with this astral body a bit. If it transcended the physical body, it should also have various degrees of transcendence over the physical world. This had already been demonstrated by flying through the roof, so to speak, but I had never experimented with any slow deliberate effort. The door to my fraternity bedroom was as good a place as any to begin the test.

I walked up to it, and stuck my hand right through it with no effort. Right through it, I tell you! Okay, how about a leg? Bingo! I then walked right through that door, stopping with my head to look into the wood of the door, which appeared like cork material. This should not have surprised me, since I had popped through the roof so many times before. My room was at the end of the hallway before the upstairs landing. As I looked down the 60 foot hall, it appeared twice as long as normal. I started to walk toward the landing. Why don't I see anybody around? How can I verify that this is real? As I got to the landing, an answer came to me. The message blackboard at the top of the stairs had two messages. "Jonathan, call your mother in Houston" and "James, Shirley called and she is angry" (actually another word for angry was used. It was a college fraternity house). "That's it!" I thought. "I will return to my body and check the message board in the normal physical realm."

I was feeling a lot of energy on this sojourn, and probably could have flown to Jupiter; but I wanted to get back and verify what I had seen on the message blackboard. So, I closed my eyes, relaxed, and gently willed myself back into my body. I woke up still drowsy. This was unusual. Nonetheless, I quickly got up to go to the message board before anyone erased what might be there. When I got to it, I saw the message for Jonathan to call his mom in Houston, but I did not see the one to James about his girlfriend, Shirley. Again, I had some confirmation like the experience with my dad's car two weeks earlier, but it was not exactly accurate. However, I asked James the next time I saw him if Shirley was mad at him?

"How did you know?" he asked. "I forgot to meet her with her parents in Austin last night. Man, I really screwed up. Did you run into her? I tried calling her earlier."

I didn't know exactly what to say, so I told him the truth ... well, most of it. "No, I haven't seen her, James. I just thought I saw a message about it on the blackboard."

He answered, "Oh, yeah. Litton wrote that this morning. He ran into her at the SUB [Student Union Building] earlier today, and said she was steaming."

I said, "Man, what a drag. Well, I hope it works out okay."

"Sure, thanks. It's not like it's the first time, and it won't be the last," he chuckled.

I nodded and gave a token laugh, also. "Oh, well. See you later, man."

"Okay, see you," he replied.

We had a big party at the fraternity house that night. I forgot my confusion and spiritual quest for a while. James and Shirley were back together, the music was great, the laughter was high, and all seemed right with the world.

When I went to bed that night, the party dwindled and I reflected back on the conflicting information from my astral trip earlier that day. I wondered if I had seen the message about James and Shirley earlier in the day before the mediation, and it just appeared to me on the board as a dream. However, the message to Jonathan was taken at 3:00, and I had been in my room since 2:00, so I couldn't have seen that one before the astral trip. That was solid confirmation. Yes, indeed, things were really looking up. I supposed that partial confirmation was better than none, but I sure would have liked something more definitive. No problem. I was about to get that in karate. It wouldn't be in the astral realm. It would be in the real karate world of strikes and blocks. But it was surely to be a power that manifested from a spiritual kingdom.

Chapter 3

Waterfalls, Serpent Energy, and Martial Arts

I had taken a few karate lessons during Free University, a group of extra-curricular activities available to students designed to broaden their base of experience. Boy, did that goal get achieved in my case. The karate lessons themselves were good, but what became most important was my personal introduction to a master of the arts who would frequent the class. Chin was a kind and wise man. He and I began a dialog about metaphysics and eastern philosophies. He had a sophisticated grasp of how they are interrelated with the martial arts.

At first, I thought his grasp of English was not so sophisticated. "The open hand life will not close if good learning is," were the first words he ever spoke to me. My eyes drifted with total confusion as I thought about what he had just said.

After smiling as if I understood, I somehow sur-
mised he meant to say that learning well in karate can open up a lot of truths about life, or something like that. After a few more meetings at the
lessons, either his English improved rapidly, or
he was messing with me at our introduction. He
suggested we work together on some more advanced spiritual aspects of the martial arts. Of
course, I was curious, and willing to increase my
knowledge about this new universe I was discov-
ering. We scheduled to meet in the yard at his
apartment complex in Austin. This was only about
a twenty-five minute drive from the University in
Georgetown.

The first session was almost all talk. About
Buddha and Buddhism. The Dalai Lama and
Avalokitesvara. About the illusion of Maya in
Hinduism. The tides of the ocean and the tides of
life. "Water defeats all who struggle against it by
yielding to their struggle." About rolling with the
punches in karate and rolling with the blows of
life. "Running with a rolling rock is better than
running against it." About sensing the spiritual
lessons behind those blows. This was the important thing about the challenge of life as it was
about the inner discipline of the martial arts. To
control the mind is to control the body in karate.
To control the mind is to control life. To focus a

blow on a brick or on an opponent is to focus a blow against ignorance, what the Hindus call karma. His mention of Hinduism surprised me, because the martial arts as we know them in the west are generally associated more with Buddhism, especially the Shaolin forms. This just showed me how broad Chin's grasp was on life and the spiritual aspects of the martial arts.

I asked, "But isn't karma the effect of an earlier cause? I do not understand how that can be ignorance. I thought ignorance relates more to Maya. Besides, if I control everything, am I not interfering with these spiritual laws."

He stood up and walked over to where he had two cement bricks suspended between two stacks of bricks. He said, "I now become one with brick. I offend not. It does not hurt me." He turned to them and bowed. With a simple hammer fist and a "Keai," they crumbled. He bowed to the shattered pile of bricks. He turned to me and spoke again, "Karma comes from ignorance. You make cause without knowing why. Effect comes back to you. You fail in law of karma with ignorance."

After this demonstration, I decided I would not speak everything that came across my mind, such as, 'Why not just get out of the way of a rolling rock?' He seemed gentle and passive, but I really did not wish to irritate him. I gathered he was saying that enlightenment helps us to spin off karmic debt, and ignorance causes us to take on more to be dealt with now or later, perhaps in another life. Pretty basic, but sometimes the basics need to be heard several times in order to be grasped in their full profundity. In this case, they hit home hard enough to shatter bricks.

However, I did ask further, "But all karma was not created in ignorance. A slave master who reincarnates as a slave knew at the time that his crimes against his fellow men were wrong. A man who accumulates wealth by drugs, murder, or some other criminal activity knows it is wrong. Everybody has heard that the love of money is the root of all evil. You don't see these wrong things as ignorance, do you?"

He answered, "Problem with question is this. You focus on right and wrong. These bad people you speak of, they know they do bad. But they do not know of better places to be."

"You mean higher spiritual realms?" I asked.

He answered, "Yes, Mark, Yes. They too are ignorant. They miss great joy by their greedy lust. This lesson they must learn."

I asked, "What do you mean by the focus on right and wrong? If that is erroneous thinking, then how do these people know that they are doing wrong?"

He replied almost laughing, "Aha! No absolutes. No right and wrong. You must understand. All is one. There is proper action in love. There is good and bad behavior; but it is only good for spiritual growth. Not in the way of right or wrong."

This reminded me a bit of the discussions with Stan about the universe already being perfect, and therefore evil was just an illusion, perhaps a part of the Hindus' Maya. However, I was still a bit confused. The atrocities of Hitler and Stalin and so many tyrants throughout mankind's bloody history surely must be seen as evil or wrong, and not just as bad behavior. I asked Chin about this.

He answered, "The injustice you see. All of it. This is karma working magic. All is done for growth to higher self. Evolution for mankind and growth for each person. This for both the tyrant and the suffering peasant, the disciple and the master. Hitler will love same as Buddha someday."

This helped, but I was puzzled, so I said, "But if these appearances of injustice are for the spiritual growth of each person and for mankind's evolution, why should we try to control life? Shouldn't we just take what comes and work off our karma?"

He leaped with joy at these questions, and

said, "Great! Great! Mark, so, so good! Question is the answer. The perfect, perfect answer. Taking what comes. This is proper control. The water yields! Roll with the punches. Swim with tide. Yield and control. Yield and control."

I began to grasp the metaphysical paradox which he was trying to teach me. I even began to see the different levels to this truth. The more accepting we are of life's events, the more control we will have over them. The more we suppress our individual ego, the greater our spiritual power will be. Only when we become one with the universe will we truly realize our individual potential. It seemed irrational, but I was learning that the ultimate truth of the universe must also be the ultimate paradox. Perhaps when I reached a state when I was no longer ignorant, this would seem no longer so paradoxical.

I was utterly disappointed when he said, "You now ready for come back next week. Same time, same channel." It just cracked him up to say that. "We finish for today. Good-bye. Safe journey to George's Town. I see you at University Class. Do not forget daily practice on defense techniques." He smiled warmly, bowed, and turned away.

"That's George ... town," I spoke as he walked away to his apartment and disappeared around the corner. I stood there deciding whether it was a train or a semi that had just run over me. As I walked back to my car, I wondered if Chin would end next week's lesson so suddenly. Well, it would end abruptly, but I would be the one walking away.

When I arrived the following week, Chin was already waiting in the yard. He waved joyfully as I pulled into a parking space. He was wearing a bandanna around his neck. As I approached, he waved for me to hurry over. "Mark. Mark. Come. Here. This goes around your eyes today." He removed the bandanna and it became my blindfold. "Make sure you cannot see."

"I can't, Chin," I chuckled. "What is this all about?"

"This, Mark, is about yielding to control. Now, get into a shallow horse stance. Hands in open hand punching ready position."

I spread my feet about 50% greater than shoulders' width, and bent my knees into a shallow crouch, with hands pulled back and open at my belt-line. "Chin, am I going to warm up blindfolded today?" I asked.

He replied, "No warm-up today. You already limber. You are like rubber, more than any American I know. You are ready for today. Now, just block my punches to your face."

I protested, "What? I can't even see. How will I ..." Whap. I felt a soft but slightly stinging strike to my left cheek. "Hey, Chin. Hold on a minute."

Chin interrupted me. "No talk. Just relax and feel when and where I will strike. Karate is more than what you see. Balance is more than just body. Balance is also in mind and soul. You see when you feel."

I gave a worried laugh and said, "Okay, but please no groin strikes. I have a feeling I might not block all of your strikes during this exercise and I might want children someday."

He responded, "Not to worry. Only high strikes to block today."

Whap. Another sting to the left cheek. I waited for this 'feeling' I was supposed to have. Just as I was about to throw a high block on the right side, another sting to my left cheek. "Chin, you are making this easier if you are going to strike the same place every time." Whap. Whap. A slight sting on top of my head and then to my right shoulder. There went my same-place theory.

He spoke, "Okay, Mark. Keep blindfold on and sit."

I sat down on the grass with my legs crossed. I spoke up, "Chin, I think I know what you must be trying to do, but I am not sure I am ready for this." I must have looked like an idiot sitting there talking to him with this bandanna across my eyes.

"No more talk, now," he responded. "Just relax now and tell me when you feel my hand next to your head."

I relaxed as though I was going to meditate. About twenty seconds later I 'felt' the warmth of his hand near my right temple and spoke up, "Are you near my head now, Chin? I think I feel something." I might have also seen a change in light through the blindfold as the hand came nearer, but I cannot be sure.

"Yes, Mark, yes. You are yielding to higher control. Now I go faster, and you block. But still slowly. Still slowly."

This time I felt something nearing the front of my face and slowly but firmly threw a high center block to sweep it away. Sure enough, my wrist made contact with his forearm. Not the best of blocks, but quite acceptable for a blind man. I then threw a rising block with the other arm as I felt my hair rustled by an approaching strike, again in slow motion. I could not tell if it was heat, sound, light, or motion that I was detecting, but it was certainly a new experience for me since I was not doing these slow-mo blocks by sight. I began to wonder if it was even more than something my ordinary senses could detect.

Chin spoke up with, "Now stand. Back in position you go."

I returned to the shallow horse open hand punching stance. Again, I felt a slowly approaching strike to my nose, and swept it away with a high center block. Suddenly, I felt an exhilaration flowing through my body. I was almost dizzy from the high. I quickly threw a left rising block. Contact! Then a down block and contact. Then a right mid-center block, followed by a left stick block, re-cocking my hands every time. Contact.! Contact! Each block connected with an approaching strike. Wow! But then ... Something felt terribly wrong about all of this. I was slightly nauseous, and felt ever so fearful. It was that familiar dread of a presence, but it was just too strong this time for me to even think about coping with it.

I ripped off the blindfold, and said, "Chin, this just can't be. How was that possible?" I felt almost desperate. Confusion. Fear. Even anger. "I can't do this, Chin. I just can't!"

He looked at me puzzled and said, "Mark, you are white as a ghost sheet." I had no idea where he got that expression, but as ridiculous as it was, I couldn't even laugh. I was so nervous about what had just happened that I began to shiver.

I said, "Chin, I just let those blocks get thrown. I don't even feel as though I did it myself."

I had enough experience with astral projection to imagine I could have left my body while another 'being' inhabited it for a few seconds, as ridiculous as I knew that really was. It was a great feat to assemble that blocking combination blindfolded, but I felt confused about who or what was performing the art. My imagination was running wild and getting the best of me. I was scared, very scared.

"Chin, I'm sorry. I don't know what's wrong with me, but that was just too much." I was anxious and in a hurry, though I had no idea why.

He responded, "Mark. All is well. You were yielding. You controlled the strikes by giving in to greater self. Yield to control. Seek the warrior's heart."

I retorted, "No, Chin. I'm sorry. I'm so sorry. Something is really upsetting me. I was not in control at all, and that scares me. I don't know what's wrong, but, well, I'm sorry. I just can't do this. I ... have to go." I handed him the bandanna I had been holding this whole time. I turned and began walking toward my car.

Chin tried to call me back, "Mark, wait."

I turned but kept moving toward the car. "Chin, listen, I'll see ya. Man. I wish I knew what's going on here. It's not you, okay? I feel bad about this. I really do. I mean, thanks for your help and all, but this just doesn't feel right."

He smiled his warm smile, waved kindly, and simply said, "See ya. Good-bye, my friend."

I felt terrible about leaving him there. I knew he was genuinely fond of me and our friendship had grown to mean a lot to both of us, but I was just so disturbed, and I didn't even know by what. It was bizarre and absurd, and to this day, I am not certain why I was so fearful, but I have some pretty solid theories which I will share later. I felt as if something a thousand times larger than me had somehow deceived me. I knew it was most likely my stupid, relentless fear that emerged in the presence of spiritual greatness, but this time was just too much for me. I had to admit it. I just couldn't handle it.

Chin never tried to call me. He was too polite to risk the appearance of intrusion. My fear made me insensitive, and I never called him. I still can't believe I just cut off our relationship like that, but it only demonstrates how deeply disturbing that day had been. A month later, I went to one last Free University karate lesson. I found myself looking for him, but he was not there. I never saw him again. Except for a few exercises and defense techniques, I gave up karate until a few years ago. Now I enjoy it again along with my two sons, but it is quite different. Chin was a kind man. I hope he is well. I hope the singular Truth of the universe is alive in his heart.

The remaining months of my sophomore year were somewhat uneventful as far as personal psychic discoveries. I did have some interesting astral journeys, but no more confirmation experiences. Mostly flying dreams, which were a lot of fun. A couple of times I went to some place that looked like Greek ruins or something. There were books open on stone pedestals everywhere. I never succeeded in focusing enough to read these books. Once I found one open to some Greek. I recognized the letters from science and fraternity initiation requirements, but I could not read it. There was a cross on the opposite page. Interesting but no big deal. Things like that just kept my appetite whetted for more.

I do remember a most unusual nightmarish astral projection. I awoke from an afternoon nap/meditation to see the sunlight streaking in my window and took a 'flight' around the campus. It was exhilarating and fun as always, but the initial rush was fading. The level of thrill was less satisfying. I decided to experiment, since I felt some control that day. I flew back into my room and went to my sanctum mirror to see if there was a reflection of this astral body in which I was flying around the campus. I saw myself in the mirror, and the reflection then began to grow hair all over its face. It quickly became contorted and changed into a hideous monster, mockingly laughing, teeth glaring, and eyes burning with fire. I was petrified, and awoke on my bed with a start. I hoped this was not the kind of self-reflection and personal growth that the AMO had in mind. If this represented the core essence of my higher self, I was not so certain I wanted to release him. How many more of these adrenaline shocks could my heart take? Those astral trips were just not turning out to be as much fun as they used to be.

I also kept up with my weekly AMO lessons. They were interesting, but there were no earth shattering experiences. Occasionally, I would get that now very familiar uneasy feeling. I came to accept that as the presence of an ascended master, obviously one associated with AMO.

One night I was deep in study in front of my sanctum altar. George, a pre-dental student, was serving as fraternity house manager. He and I often played tennis together. This night he thought I was gone. He used his master key to open my locked door so he could borrow my tennis racket. I said he could do that anytime. As I have mentioned, it was a great bunch of guys, and we could all trust each other like that. I did not realize how entranced I became during my AMO lessons until this first interruption. I was very disoriented when the door opened. For a moment, I did not even remember where I was.

George was really embarrassed and apologetic. He said, "Mark, man, I am really sorry. I knocked on your door. Didn't you hear? I thought you were gone. I, uh ... just wanted to borrow your racket." He couldn't help but stare at this bizarre sight, especially finding it in a bedroom of our fraternity house.

I got it together enough to reply, "Yeah, sure. It's okay, George. It's in my closet. Just grab it."

He opened the closet door, grabbed the racket as he said, "Okay, thanks. Man, I'm sorry."

"It's okay. Really. Don't worry about it." I wanted to crack up now. What was he thinking? George loved David Bowie, and that was about as far from center as he would ever get. He was an All-American college-Joe body-builder jock type. He must have been completely baffled by this vision before him. After he shut the door, I just had to laugh. This was ridiculous, hilarious, but also troublesome. I thought, "I guess everyone will know now."

I spoke out loud to myself a sarcastic,

"Great." I looked disappointingly at the idiot in the mirror and stopped the lesson for the night. I then turned the sanctum altar back into a college study desk.

This is just great. Now I will be revealed as a warlock or something. I will be taken out of office and banned from the fraternity. Then, someday I will probably fall asleep on a plane, forget to change gates, take the wrong route, and end up in Salem, where George's tale of my evil will have been discovered, and then they will burn me as a witch. Well, hang on now. I'm just a little nervous. Surely it's not that bad. But ... it's pretty bad.

Actually, I never heard about the incident from anybody else, so I guess good ol' George was too freaked out to talk to anybody about it. He did bring it up with me the next day.

"Hey, Mark, I'm sorry about interrupting your weird stuff last night" (he used another word for stuff - it was a college fraternity house). "It's none of my business, but what were you doing? I need to tell you it was creepy in there."

I was sarcastically thinking that this was really going to be a swell discussion. Against my better judgment, but sensing no alternative, trying to sound innocent, I then asked, "What do you mean?"

He answered, "Man, was that like witchcraft or something? I mean, it felt really strange in there."

I responded and chuckled, "No, it's not witchcraft. I was just studying some stuff. I sometimes do it by candlelight because the mood helps me memorize the material better."

George pushed a bit. "But what were you studying. Man, I'll tell you again, it felt really strange in there."

Pushing my luck, I just came out and asked him, "What do you mean, 'It felt strange'?"

He answered, "I don't know. Like witches and Satan and stuff."

I cracked up and repeated in mockery, "Witches and Satan and stuff? Come on, George. Doesn't that seem a little ridiculous?"

I could tell he was ready for this discussion to end now that it was just starting. This stuff was too far beyond listening to David Bowie, and 'Major Tom' was as distant as George ever wanted to venture from earth. So he said, "I don't know. It just felt, well, ominous."

I responded, "George, it was probably just the lighting and all. Maybe sort of set a mood. Like I said, it just helps me memorize better." I did not want to discuss what I was studying or mention anything about the psychic powers I was developing. I think George knew that whatever I was doing, I was not excited about sharing it with anybody.

He said, "Yeah, that was probably it. Well, it was intense anyway. Maybe I should try studying Organic Chemistry that way. Must just be the lighting, huh?"

I could tell he didn't mean it. This little conversation had made me more aware that there must be some universal fear about being in the presence of ascended masters, or even humans who had died and were inhabiting our spheres of evolutionary meditation. I must have been entertaining them in my room that night, even though it did not feel that way at the time. I wondered if I was finally becoming more accustomed to their presence and if I was starting to conquer the fear-factor. The answer was 'No' as summertime would reveal.

I was at the peak of optimism when my sophomore year ended. School was going great. I was focused on going to med. school. I had made the Dean's Academic List that year. I was elected to serve as president of my fraternity for the upcoming autumn term of my junior year. I was also elected to the Community Life Council of the University. My own psychic growth was also promising. I was gaining control of astral projection, yoga, and meditation. The AMO lessons were not always interesting, but they were often associated with a spiritual presence of hidden power. That was exciting, and I hoped to tap into that power for my own use as arcane knowledge and proficiency increased. The secrets of the universe seemed one lesson, one meditation, one yoga session, one astral trip away; but, the peace I was after was not yet embraced. I never could get a firm grip on it. I hoped that a summer in Austin would provide that.

I signed up for 8 hours of advanced Calculus at the University of Texas in Austin. They were supposed to have this super mathematics department, and I thought it would be nice to give it a try. My parents were kind enough to cover this summer venture, so off I went. I shared an apartment with Nick, Jay, Tim, and Neil, a friend of Nick's.

Jay turned me on to a kundalini ashram in Austin near 'the Drag.' 'The Drag' was a super cool portion of Guadeloupe Street close to UT. There were 'head' shops to shame Greenwich Village, and sidewalk vendors of every craft in the world. Wandering about were representatives of pantheism and every major multi-theistic and religion, and one could engage in philosophical dialogue 24 hours a day, seven days a week. This was an appropriate proximity for a kundalini ashram, a beacon to wandering seekers.

Kundalini is a form of yoga that requires enormous physical and mental discipline. It involves a process known as fire-breathing. This is rapid super-oxygenation accomplished by quick bursts of powerful in- and exhalations. It was usually performed in the lotus position with arms raised at 45 degree angles. I remember how mine would ache with exhaustion as post-fire-breathing chants would go on for almost an hour. "Sa Ta Nom Ma," we would repeat over and over, roughly meaning, "Truth is its name" or "Truth is the name of the Mother life-giving Force." Or, we might also repeat, "Ek Ong Kar Siri Sat Nom Wah Guru." This meant something like, "Greetings with truth, Wise Guru," addressed to the divine inner child lying dormant within each of us as the higher self.

The strenuous physical exercise of difficult stretches and contorted positions, combined with breathing techniques, chanting, and meditation, were meant to raise the serpent energy within the chakras of the body. The kundalini energy. Legend has it that many who have encountered the serpent have lost their sanity due to the intensity of its presence. But I knew I was safe under the guidance of a great yogi master from India. I had

my introductory audience with him after a few
visits to the ashram after which my sincerity was
judged worthy.

When I entered the room where the guru/
master sat as motionless as I have ever seen anyone sit, I knew I was face to face with a great power.
It was that same cosmic power I wanted to harness and master. It was evident that this man
seated in front of me had done so, and I believed
the peace I felt close to embracing was almost
within my permanent grasp.

And yet, something hit me as I entered that
room. I couldn't believe it! That burdensome, ever-
present, annoying, and disgusting fear. Why was
the fear-factor so overwhelming now in the presence of this disciplined, loving man who would help
show me the way to truth, enlightenment, and the
peace I so coveted? Sweat almost broke out on my
brow as I fought to stay free of anxiety. I thought,
"Why do these fears always plague me when I am
getting closer and closer to the truth?"

The kundalini master opened his eyes from
a deep trance and looked up to meet my eager
stare. When our eyes met, I nearly fell to the floor
as my knees weakened.

He hinted at a smile and said, "So, you want
to learn the art of deliverance?"

I replied, "Yes, Master."

"A man who can lift a thousand pounds does not impress me, but a man who can sit still does impress me. Do you know what I mean?"

I blankly stared at those eyes of fire.

"You must become dead to yourself in order to know yourself. You must die in order to live. A dead man does not move. Does he?"

"No, Master."

"You know the Bible, so popular in this country, speaks of dying to oneself. The disciples of their Christ yielded to Him to die so that they could live. You must do the same with he who speaks to you now. Know, however, that in the end, I am not your Master." He tilted his head slightly down, gazed even more intensely into my eyes, as if that were possible. He pointed his finger directly at me and said, "No, I am not your Master. You are."

"Sir, I understand."

He then smiled more openly, and said, "I know you do. Now go join the class for today. Make sure to come tomorrow. I am teaching a very special class."

"Thank-you. I will."

I left the room, joined the class which was just starting. I couldn't wait until tomorrow's 'very special class.'

It was pouring down rain in Austin the next

night. One of those blustery, dangerous, could-be-a-tornado-coming kind of a Texas storm. If I had believed in demons, I would have thought they were creating this foul weather to prevent me from getting to kundalini class that night, because it promised to be a step toward enlightenment and ultimate peace. Jay was as determined as I was, and we ventured out in my blue Opel Kadette, lights on, wipers screaming, and clipping at about 10 mph.

We arrived a bit late, but the insight and kindness of the ashram master had allowed extra time for everyone to arrive. There were some UT students who were involved in these sessions as part of their curriculum for a religion course, so they were relieved to know that the storm had not made them late. As the lightning crackled and the thunder rolled and the wind and water smashed against the window outside, the storm inside was just about to begin.

Our guru said, "Everyone please settle down, and obtain lotus position on the floor. Please. Sit. Sit." He paused and then said, "It seems the forces of weather are testing your hearts tonight. Congratulations on your presence. May it be a journey worth your trouble."

We engaged in the most difficult physical workout yet to be dispensed at the ashram. Most of the students were as wet with perspiration as if they were standing in the storm raging outside. We were then taken through a very thorough relaxation technique similar to the one I had experienced at church camp, but more detailed. We were told to mentally empty individual portions of the body of all negative energy, and to replace it with light. We worked through each toe, finger, foot, hand, ankle, etc. until a wave of positive light-like life-giving energy was ebbing up and down our bodies. We went through each chakra energy center and stimulated it through chanting and meditation, progressing up the spine until we hit the highest chakra, which was actually located just above the head. We were taught that when it is stimulated enough, this gives the impression of a halo as depicted in ancient paintings of holy men.

We then went to our backs on the floor and focused on the third eye, a place just at or above the bridge of the nose. Believe me, after an intense yoga workout and fire-breathing, focusing your eyes on that spot with eyes closed was an absolutely dizzying euphoria. As we were lying on the floor, seeking to contact the divine guru, the perfect inner child within each of us, the Master went about the room. At each person, he knelt on the floor above their heads, and touched the third eye with his index finger. My turn came, and I knew as he knelt above my head.

When his finger landed on my forehead, I thought I must have been hit by some of that lightening flashing through the night sky over Austin. An electric wave went through my body and a shock wave went through my mind. A brief moment of panic and resistance was followed by total relaxation. For several minutes, I was one with the Master who had sparked my cosmic consciousness. This at-one-ment spread through the room to the other students, and then into the entire universe. I then felt a total peace for a few seconds, but anxiety struck as I thought I was losing my own identity. I opened my eyes, and the trance was broken enough that I could relax. I felt exhausted but at ease again. I closed my eyes, and fell asleep. It was deep and recuperative, though it was only about 15 minutes. As I came to, I sat up and looked around the room at others who had obviously experienced something similar to me. When I made eye contact with any of them, we would smile at each other as if to mentally utter a big, fat, "Wow! That was really something. Wasn't it?"

On our ride back to our apartment that night, Jay and I were rather subdued. It was still raining pretty hard, but the squall line and the brunt of the storm had past. We shared our experiences and found them to be very similar.

"What do you think?" I asked.

"I think that guru has a lot of power," responded Jay.

"No kidding! And he was spreading some around tonight wasn't he?"

Jay nodded and said, "Yes. I got my share."

I decided to speak up about my panic. "Jay, I've got to tell you, man, I had a moment there where I was a bit shaken up. I mean, I hate to admit it, but I got really scared, like I was losing myself or something. I know that is the goal, but it felt like I was just going too fast into a world I'm not quite ready for. I guess it's the stinking fear factor again."

I was glad to find out that Jay had the same feelings. "Mark, I felt the same way. That is what's good about AMO. Sometimes it seems boring, but the pace somehow seems safer."

I responded, "Well, the exercises are good. I just might lighten up on the other aspects of kundalini for a while. You gonna go back tomorrow?"

"Of course." We both laughed.

"Yeah. Me, too."

I went to sleep that night, feeling closer than ever before to making a new step in the direction of my spiritual evolution. I was becoming more comfortable with the idea of an impersonal creative Force behind the universe, and not the infinite personal God of my Christian childhood. I was beginning to accept my eventual existence in the godhead as one with the universe. The transition away from individual ego and into cosmic consciousness finally seemed plausible. But these philosophical views were to be shaken the very next afternoon.

I refused to believe what was happening, but that refusal did not change the facts. "Is this really how I am going to die?" I thought. My heart was pounding with adrenaline and my eyes were darting around seeking an escape. I remember how blue the central Texas sky was that day I thought was to be my last. What a contrast it was to the electrical storm from the previous night spent at the ashram.

As a result of the heavy rains, lake engineers had increased the spillway flow over the top of the dam from the lake upon which Timothy and I were sailing our two-man craft. Apparently, they had not moved the warning buoys further out to indicate the increased surface current in the lake toward the dam. We had been captured by the current and could not tack free. The Colorado River was raging below the dam and it grew louder as we approached the spillway.

"Mark, are we going over this dam?" Timothy asked in surprisingly calm surrender. He had a remarkably funny talent for understatement, but I wasn't laughing very hard.

"It looks that way," I replied as my words were lost to the crashing roar of the water on the other side of the dam. My last thought of escape was to try and jump free of the turbulence below the dam. If I survived the impact of the fall, then at least I might be capable of getting to shore or grabbing onto what might be left of the sailboat.

As we plunged over the spillway, my attempt to jump free failed. I found myself trapped in the undercurrent beneath the dam. I struggled to break free but my efforts were futile, in spite of my being a strong swimmer. Then I remembered a whitewater trick one could use in case of being dumped in such waters (besides sailing over dams, I was also an avid canoeist). 'Protect your head, relax, and hope the current will eventually carry you to the calmer waters.' This also gives you a longer use of that last breath more than struggling would allow. It is tempting to ignore this method

112

when you find yourself below tons of raging foam.

I remember crying out with all the strength of my mind, "God, help me. I am not ready to die." I might have struggled myself to death, except ... a remarkable thing happened. Suddenly, I felt a very personal, very real, and calming presence. For a few moments, I forgot that I no longer believed in my personal God of earlier days. I forgot this because now I found myself praying to Him. Somehow, an impersonal oversoul of planetary consciousness just would not do in this circumstance. At that particular time, I was not thinking of the New Age dawning upon Mother Earth. I received the ability to relax as a gift that day. I stopped struggling and was eventually carried away from the black back current beneath the dam. As my chest was burning for oxygen, I wrestled to the surface and gasped, devouring the sweetest air I have ever tasted. I swam vigorously until I knew I was free of the eddy back-drawing toward the dam.

Timothy had been thrown free of this trouble. He was on the rear of the craft when we went over, and the jerk of the falling water caught the front of the boat and catapulted him to safer waters, but not without a price. The force of the spill water was so powerful that it had snapped the mast of the sailboat, which came tearing into his leg. He was almost impaled. He suffered more bruises than I did as well because he was thrown into more shallow waters; but, he had been spared the near-drowning ordeal.

Timothy looked at me with astonished relief. "Where have you been? Are you okay?" he asked. Apparently he had been up for quite some time, which meant I had been under for quite some time. It is quite probable that the excellent conditioning and breathing techniques from the ashram had given me just enough edge to last so long beneath the water's surface. There could have been grace of another kind involved as well.

I had to pause between words as I was still catching my breath. "I'm okay, Tim. How 'bout you?"

"I think so." He climbed out of the water, and the blood spilling down his legs was most disconcerting. We were relieved when closer inspection revealed wounds that could be salvaged by a few stitches.

There was a very sweet, old, wise-looking black man fishing below the dam who had witnessed this whole drama. He had been watching with some curiosity, naturally, and finally spoke as we were resting near him on the bank.

"Excuse me, boys; but if ya'll meant to take

that ride, then I'm gonna have to call you stupid," he joked with us.

He had a wonderful smile, and I just had to chuckle. "No, sir," I said with a soft laugh. "That was not our plan."

He responded, "Well, then, it seems Jesus wasn't ready for you to head on. He must have an interest in sparing your lives."

Now, ordinarily, I enjoyed debating philosophy with a Christian, especially when the name of Jesus was evoked as if He were uniquely divine above the rest of us; but, I just wasn't in the mood at that particular time. Besides, this man was the one calmly enjoying the afternoon with his reassuring smile, and an impressive string of catfish. I was the one soaking wet, battered and bruised, whose heart rate was just now slowing to 100. It did not appear that I had a knowledge of the ultimate truth greater than the fisherman. I began to wish that my last twenty-four hours had been spent with him.

However, I was yet learning that appearances are deceiving. Maya, the illusion of this world. My bruised body wanted to soak in a hot tub. My bruised pride held onto this present circumstance as Maya. I pumped myself back up, thinking, "This old fisherman will encounter such growing experiences as these in his next lifetime. Perhaps this time around he is just learning to relax and observe, a sort of Zen approach to life. Yes. That must be it. I just temporarily fell back into that old mechanistic Christianity thing under the stress of the fear I felt beneath the dam. I am still growing. I am still evolving. I am still progressing on my path to perfection. Everything is fine and enlightenment is on schedule."

Nonetheless, I skipped my kundalini yoga session at the ashram that night. In fact, I decided to engage in the less intense and more simple hatha yoga from then on. As for studies into the mystical, I stuck only to my AMO lessons for a while. I never saw the ashram again. I was beginning to question my ability to stick with my spiritual journey when things got a little rough. First, I had abandoned Chin and his spirit karate, and now kundalini. However, I knew that each path must be individually chosen and mapped out. I just hadn't found the right combination of New Age disciplines yet. I kept repeating to myself, "Patience. All is well. Peace will come." Though it remained illusive, my hopes for the ultimate end to this quest stayed strong. I still believed that 'You shall know all' was appropriate to what I maintained would be my destiny. Yet shall I forge ahead.

Chapter 4

Physics, Music, and Human Nature

Not only was this peace for which I grew more hungry remaining illusive, my life was also being accompanied by a growing uneasiness. I assumed this was due to my impatience for enlightenment. However, I was also having difficulty feeling as grounded about my perceptions of reality as I had felt a couple of years earlier. Whatever the reason, my quest for cosmic consciousness had begun to consume me. I was fully aware of this, and accepted that such obsession was necessary to achieve any great thing in life. And what could be greater than acquiring total enlightenment? What more could I accomplish in life than to become an ascended master? What knowledge could be more important than ultimate truth?

Shortly after returning to school, I had one of those 'til-almost-dawn discussions with Les, a close friend of Olan's. I had also known Les from high school, but had never really gotten to know him very well, even though I thought he was a nice and sincere fellow. He was a very bright guy as well, a straight-A student. He had become a Jesus freak his first two years of college and Olan wanted me to help set him straight.

He was a decent tennis player and we played a full match one night in mid-October of 1975. After the last game, we stayed at the courts talking about religion and philosophy. By 2:00 a.m., I realized I had just given my first New Age sermon, basically summing up the basics of my belief system. I reflected back on Stan's potato chip association with God as I pointed to the fence around the courts in response to Les' question, "Okay, Mark, who or what is God, then?"

"Les," I said. "This. This fence is God. Not because it is superior to you or me or anything else, but because it is a part of the universe. God is all that is, and there is a single force, a single creative energy behind it all. The universe is God, and God is the universe. It is like we are all parts of one gigantic mind, which is singular and imper-sonal in nature. The word that best describes it is pantheism. It comes from the word pantheos - the temple of the gods. All the universe is really this temple, and we are all the gods inhabiting this temple we call the universe. But there is more to it than just the material world. There are many planes and dimensions of existence. I guess you have heard the Flatland story, where all the creatures are two-dimensional. If a sphere comes along and slides up and down in their two-dimensional plane, it just appears to be a circle changing size. Just as the circles in Flatland had difficulty understanding the total concept of a sphere, so do we three-dimensional beings have difficulty comprehending there is more to us. But what is really exciting about all of this is that we are already more. We are already gods. We are already one with the universe. We simply must bring our own thinking into line with this reality. This is what is meant by nirvana, going clear, or cosmic consciousness. This is achieved by re-incarnation, coming back to this earth-plane over and over until you escape your karmic debt, or karma. Karma is the effect you receive from one of your consciousness causes. Some gurus call good deeds karma yoga, because they help to spin off the debt you have to the universe. When all the debt is paid, you escape this plane of consciousness and move on into the status of an ascended master, eventually to escape the need for physical embodiment. There are different theories on how each person progresses after that, but the main point is that everyone eventually achieves perfect blissful union with the universe, although I am not exactly sure what that means just yet. I guess if I knew, I would have already achieved it. We are created in the image of God, so we are all mini-gods walking around on this planet. What we think and say have actual effects on reality, because the same creative force of the universe is within each one of us. Not only is our personal reality shaped by our words and thoughts, but that of our dear sweet earth is also. The big news is that the whole planet is preparing for a major shift in consciousness and evolution. You and I sitting here talking about this mark only the beginning of a wildfire of harmonizing energy that will peak at about the turn of the century, nearing the time when the race will be catapulted into its next evolutionary species stage. Those who are not prepared, especially people like the ones who believe in a single personal God, will be made ready by education with ascended masters or whatever. I have to admit I am not quite sure about what I have heard regarding the old-time religion people, but they will eventually be enlightened to understand the beautiful growth in planetary consciousness, and will join the new human race as it enters the Age of Aquarius. There will still be karma to pay off and all that, but our existence will be from a new vantage point. Just as if apes would somehow become human, so will we humans become more god-like. Our physical evolution is tied into our spiritual evolution. We will understand that these ideas of categorizing things under good and evil have just been to make life convenient while we were in our present lower state of evolution. Believing in absolutes of right and wrong are like survival instincts to us, like a lioness sharing her prey with her cubs. She doesn't do that because it is the right thing to do. She does it because that is her instinct."

Les stopped me there, saying, "Now, wait a minute, the Bible says that mankind is in essence bad, and you are basically saying that mankind is in essence good. I think that is what you're saying, anyway, considering your analogy to the lioness."

I answered him, "Well, I guess I am saying that. Your potential is to do good, to become more highly evolved. If a race believes it is basically bad, it will self-fulfill its own prophecy by behaving in a way it believes it is destined to behave. We have wars and crimes and addictions and act like this fallen race of the Bible because we believe we are this fallen race of the Bible. If we believe we are to become gods, we will start acting like it. We can create and shape our own reality and stop being victims of an antiquated belief system. Evolution has gone on whether the species involved wanted it or not, and it will be the same way with the great change that is about to happen on Spaceship Earth."

Les looked at me pensively, and said, "I just don't know, Mark. A lot of what you say makes sense; but, I find it hard to picture me sitting on God's throne, or at least the throne of a god.

I replied, "I know it is a scary thing. I have had more adrenaline rushes than I care to consider throughout my recent search. But change is necessary for growth. And growth into the evolution of a higher state of consciousness is the destiny of every individual, no matter how far along they may currently be on the path to enlightenment. There is no good reason to fight it. But, also, you can take as long as you like. That is the neat thing about getting away from these false boundaries and taking charge of creating your own eternal reality. In some ways it is pretty scary, but in another way it is a lot easier. You sort of choose your own pace suited for you. And who knows better than you about what your needs are in the ultimate scheme of things?"

Les smiled as if to indicate he was starting to grasp it. He said, "Man, you are quite a salesman for this stuff."

I said, "No. The truth has a way of selling

itself. That's all." I pointed out toward Hutto Road. "Hey, look at that. The sky is getting brighter in the east. I think I'll go back to the fraternity house and get some rest." I thought that 'sky in the east' line was pretty neat, a great poetic symbolism. I was proud that I must be evolving spiritually in order to come through with lines like that. Aquarian New Age thought has infinite room for the largest of egos, so I had plenty of room to stretch mine. In a healthy and humble kind of way, of course.

Les agreed, "Yes, not a bad idea. Listen, I'll see you around ... and, thanks."

I said, "Sure. Thank-you. It was a great discussion." (As if I had allowed him a word in the last couple of hours). "I enjoyed it. Really. I'll see you later."

Olan told me a month later that Les had joined the AMO. I was so excited that I had been a part of this. To me, it symbolized the dawning truth that was spreading across the planet, and I was now more than a spectator. However, I had a long way to go. I was still just an ordinary human, ... well, at least according to certain criteria.

I had spent my summer before my junior year with four politically conservative individuals, three of them in the AMO. Jay especially influenced me into realizing that the victim-status and class-hatred thinking of socialists and liberals just enslaved people. He had a very compassionate heart for the downtrodden as did I, and we had both come to realize that individual freedom was a greater gift than a welfare check, though temporary help in that form was certainly called for at times in certain cases. This seemed to fit what I was coming to believe about spiritual matters as well, even though it was odd that we were becoming more politically aligned with conservative Christians. We thought it was strange that so many people involved in spiritual truth searching were politically liberal, and that so many involved in the politics supporting personal initiative and free enterprise were religious conservatives. We just reconciled this as simple political ignorance on the part of truth students, and simple spiritual ignorance on the part of the politically conservative Christians. The important realization for me was that I best dealt with my karma by taking on the challenges of life with my own responsibility, and relying on others as little as possible. This was one more confirmation that things were falling together for me personally as far as philosophical matters were concerned.

Another brainstorm of political enlightenment was to come from my physics professor. He was a hilarious, super-energetic man, with whom most students developed a love-hate relationship. They loved his wit and personality and hated the fact that his physics courses were the most difficult in the known world. I was staying late one afternoon finishing one of his impossible lab assignments. He was rather active in politics and took that afternoon's opportunity to test the political waters with me. No doubt he was aware of my alternate delegate status in the McGovern campaign two years earlier and had heard rumors that I was now abandoning the liberal ship.

He came prancing over with his Santa Claus belly bouncing along with him, "Well Mr. Phillips, have you confirmed the realities of the known universe today? Or are you wallowing in self-pity over your plight as a mere student of physical inquiry?"

I replied, "Hello, Dr. Black. All is well at this station, sir. The true facts are firmly within my reach." He got a kick out of it when students spoke like that, and it was a real blast. I could talk to him about anything, even though it was often a humbling experience.

He let loose that enormous and contagious laughter, then said, "Fine, fine." He paused and by the way he looked at me, I could tell I was about to be grilled on something, though I had no idea what that might be. He continued, "Mr. Phillips, what do you think money is?"

Now I wondered where he could be going with this. I answered with sarcasm in my voice, "A necessary evil?"

"It's not a riddle, Mr. Phillips. However accurate that may be, what more do you think money is?"

I braced myself for a dose of humility. I answered, "It's what you can buy things with. It represents purchasing power."

Dr. Black's eyes lit up, and his eyebrows went up and down like Groucho Marx as he said, "Aha, the secret word. Power. A good physics word, Mr. Phillips. But it is not exactly accurate. A better word for money is energy. I put out a lot of energy teaching you the truths of the way the Great Architect's universe operates."

I chuckled and said, "No argument there."

"Right, right, Mr. Phillips. Then someone like your dad signs a check representative of that energy I have put forth. Then I go use that money to buy things I need to live and thrive. That money goes to, let's say, the grocer, who uses it to represent his energy put forth in running the grocery. He keeps some for himself and passes some on to the men who deliver the food. That man keeps some and passes some onto the farmer. The farmer uses the energy from the sun. Of course, in reality, there are a lot more middle men than this, but I think I have once again successfully transferred knowledge to an avid student. Crystal clear, Mr. Phillips?"

I answered, "Yes. Quite. Money is energy, even though the greedy may call it power."

He responded, "Well, do not be too hard on that definition. From my classes, you know how energy and power are closely related by equation." He paused as I nodded, reassuring him that I had grasped at least that much basic physics. He then asked, "Now, can energy be created from nothing?"

I answered confidently, "No, that would be a violation of thermodynamic laws."

"Good, good, Mr. Phillips. So when the liberals in Washington want to create a program out of thin air, where does the money, the energy to run that program come from? It cannot be created out of thin air, so the energy must be transformed, delivered from another source. That source is the most abundant supply of money in the world. The American middle class. But the liberals squeal that the rich are not paying their fair share, but it's the middle class that feels the brunt of these programs created out of thin air. If we took all of the money the rich of this country have, it would not be enough to run Washington for very long at all. Now, I want you to remember something. The money in this country is in the middle class, and that is where anybody in the government looking for funding of any kind will go to find it. Never forget that, Mr. Phillips."

I simply responded to him, "You're right. And I promise not to forget."

I had a good grasp of politics and economics and by the time this conversation occurred, I was already in Dr. Black's camp. But this helped clarify a few things for me. However, what continued in the conversation also influenced my spiritual philosophy, though I would not fully appreciate that until 13 years later. Dr. Black then got that look of interrogation on his face again and once more I braced myself.

He asked, "Now then, what is the greatest enemy of efficiency?"

I answered confidently again, "Power loss. Technically heat, or more accurately, friction."

"Very good, Mr. Phillips. Friction. Now you have a good one-word definition for taxes. Every time money changes hands from me to the grocer and on through to the farmer, friction as taxation is there to bog down the economic machine. For every dollar we send to Washington to care for a needy family, less than one dime gets to that family. This is the evil of bureaucracy. It is a big and inefficient machine, and all the best motives in the world will not make it work any better, because it cannot be done." His next line is what shook up my philosophical status quo. "Government bureaucracy does not take into account human nature, Mr. Phillips. Self-preservation does not make for service to others. The socialist system depends on human beings to more evenly distribute wealth and power. But those human beings tend to hold onto the power that comes from the bureaucratic privilege, just as the wealthy people do from whom these bureaucrats take the tax money. Both groups are humans with selfish needs. Human nature, Mr. Phillips. Human nature."

He could tell I was straining to grasp his point so he clarified further. He continued, "The average person who can make his own rules is going to fit them to his own purposes nine times out of ten. That's human nature. We are all basically selfish. It's tough to admit it, but we must have the courage to do so. Only then can we start to do something about it. When the government gets so large that it becomes necessary for departments to make up their own rules just to keep the beast alive, then human nature comes forth, and they make those rules to enhance the life of the rulemaker, not the people they are supposed to be serving. The men and women we control by the election process lose sight and control of this big, ugly, self-serving bureaucratic monster, and the people within this beast self-serve with their own rules because things have gotten too big and complex for anybody to keep checks on them. That is why centralizing power and wealth for redistribution will never work. Mark my words, communism in the eastern bloc will fail before the turn of the century. I just hope I live to see it." Many years later, Dr. Black must have seen the same news footage that we all saw as the Berlin wall came crashing down. The inefficient machine of centralization had collapsed under its own inefficiency. Dr. Black recently died, and I am sure he would say that the creature of centralization will constantly be rearing its ugly head, but that all forms will eventually crash with the death of a dictator or the overtaxed economy.

I was definitely enlightened that afternoon in the physics lab. It should come as no surprise by now, but I was more interested in the spiritual aspect of what he was saying. Interested is not exactly the right word. I was rather disturbed. What Dr. Black had to say made sense, but it did not exactly fit the model idea I had of humans as basically good, waiting for opportunities to strive to be better, to strive toward perfection to cosmic consciousness, to godhood. However, I could not let it deter my own progress. It was something I could resolve in due time. I had my own spiritual evolution to think about. I had to take care of myself. But ... hmmm, that is just what Dr. Black was saying.

In my final two years of college, my studies into the doctrines of spiritual freedom became the most important thing to me, not politics or even my majors of biology and chemistry, though I continued an academic focus toward med. school. I knew I was becoming addicted to the feelings of power that came from astral projection and the discipline of yoga. As I waned a bit in my love for science, I became more interested in the creative fine arts, because I was beginning to see them as doors into another world. Inspirations from science may have been given from ascended masters, but the focus was still on this world. The arts, especially music, took me out of this world. I began to play piano more and more, all by ear, since I had no formal training. I got some books on music theory and composition and I wrote some symphonic pieces as well as some pop-like tunes all touting the optimism of the new era dawning upon this planet. Following is one example:

"See the sun. Always rising. Always setting. Always noon.

Know the sun for what it represents to us, and maybe, oh surely,

you'll be answered very soon."
Another was:

"Each vibration has a critical point.
Sin waves revived. A mass to anoint.
The man with my thought on the ground of
the sky.
With a breath to share, all visions we sigh.
Have you asked
Why the trees really live to grow?
Surely now, you've thought of this before,
When science will be asking, 'Why?'
I AM. I AM."

These songs weren't enough. The AMO lessons weren't enough. The yoga wasn't enough. The meditation wasn't enough. The many books I had read thus far were not enough. By the time I graduated from college, I could manifest a trance-like state of meditation in which I knew I was in the presence of an ascended master. I had been engaged in some successful telekinesis experiments such as table-lifting and bending spoons. I was gaining control over my diet, my body, my mind, and my emotions. But it was still not enough. There was a priceless pearl of truth that was to be mine and I did not want anything or anybody to get in my way of having it.

The night before graduation, I was walking around campus with Reba. I wasn't exactly sure what I wanted to do at this juncture of my life, other than disappear into the Himalayas or something until I knew what I needed and wanted for the peace that surpasses all understanding. We wandered over to the FAB (Fine Arts Building). She checked the door and found that it was open.

"Come here," she said. "Play for me." She was referring to the grand piano that sat center stage in the main auditorium. She loved my piano playing and always had kind remarks about my songs and impromptu ramblings upon the ivory. I went on into the building with her.

When we entered the auditorium, it was nearly pitch black. So we carefully made our way down to the stage where the piano was propped like a gateway to the celestial. I played a variation on one of my compositions, a piece I called 'Stillness.' It was one of her favorites. It reflected the paradoxical blend of tranquillity and impatience I felt during meditation. While I was physiologically settled during my deepest encounters with the spirit world, I was most often mentally and emotionally clutching for some new grasp of esoteric knowledge that would release me from my mortal bonds. I was so often baffled after meditating because though I was calm and still, I was yet anxious for something so much more. I assumed this was the natural evolutionary urging, not of a tortured soul, but of a man striving for the spiritual greatness that was his destiny along with every other sample of his species. Man, I was really taking myself so seriously sometimes. Well, actually most of the time. Piano gave this intensity an outlet for me. (Things such as canoeing and comedy movies, especially the Peter Sellers' Pink Panther films, also gave great escapes of diversion).

Reba got a bit emotional as I played for thirty minutes non-stop that night. It was contagious. When I finished, I put my head in my hands and fought back the tears. "Reba," I said. "I have done the wrong thing here in college. I have studied the wrong things and done the wrong things. I have wasted so much time."

She responded, "Why? What do you mean? Do you think you should have studied music or what? Listen, you can always change your course."

I answered, "Maybe. I don't know. I just should have done whatever brought me closer to the truth. Music, pre-med, religion, maybe nothing at all. None of that really matters. Oh, I'm not sure. I only know that something is burning inside me that is telling me there is an ultimate truth to an ultimate reality and it can be known and had by the human mind, heart, and spirit. I want this for myself. I have spent all this time and effort at school that could have been committed to that end. 'Stillness' and losing myself in the piano makes me feel better for a while. My AMO lessons do the same, but just for a short time. Meditation helps, temporarily, but I feel just as ignorant as I did years ago when my search began. Heck, my mind is even invaded with this desire for the truth while I am watching a baseball game! What could be more captivating than that?" We both laughed.

She asked jokingly, "Do I fit in there anywhere as a decent distraction from your torment?"

I chuckled and said, "Very funny. Man, Reba, your friendship is great. You know that. I really appreciate it."

She said, "Listen, Mark, I have no doubt that whatever it is you are trying to accomplish or discover, it will eventually be your prize. Your time here isn't wasted. Your knowledge of science will fit into the grand scheme somehow, and I know you hate to hear it, but your good education here will serve you in this material world you are so busy trying to escape." We both laughed at that and then she said compassionately and with the conviction of confidence, "Mark, it may take you five, ten, twenty years, or even a lifetime. But you will have what you need and want. Believe me."

I replied, "Thanks, Reba. I have to hold on to believing that. I guess I'll continue to affirm that in my meditation and visualizations. I've got to tell you, though, sometimes I scare myself with this obsession, but I don't know any other way to nirvana."

She lightened up the atmosphere by saying, "Oh, brother. Mark, you get obsessed with everything you think and do. It sort of makes you attractive in a strange way, but it is also a pain in the neck. It's cute and sickening at the same time. Listen, your precious truth will come. Besides, think of the good things along the journey. When we met four years ago, I didn't believe in anything. Now I am a convert."

"I know. I know. My apologies."

Again, we laughed. I continued, "I just don't want anything to interfere."

She responded, "With something you're focused on? Forget it."

I hoped she was right. I was so afraid of getting caught up in the cares of this world that I would lose my way on the journey to enlightenment. As things turned out, it did not appear that medical school was going to interfere with my quest. Not for a year anyway. I was secretly glad that I did not successfully gain admission into medical school the first year after college. I could now take a year off to engage in full-time truth-searching and then go off to med. school, at which point I knew my study time for anything other than medicine would be virtually eliminated. I had one remaining year to advance as quickly as possible in my spiritual maturity toward enlightenment.

Chapter 5

Car Crashes, Avatars, and Social Collapse

After graduation, I moved to Austin thinking I might pick up a job with a pharmaceutical company or something. After a month, however, I heard the real estate market was pretty good in Nashville. That sounded like a good thing to get into for a while and I thought I might be able to do something with my music there as well. But I knew all I was really concerned with was making as much time available as possible to study and discipline myself toward eternal enlightenment. This was my only purpose for existence and was the shaping factor in all of my decisions. Nashville was as good a place as any. Furthermore, my brother John and his family were there, so off I went. I wonder if that means I went off.

I spent August with John and Carol and

their two boys. I got a book on real estate so I could take the licensing exam in September. I passed and got my license, and went to work as an affiliate broker. I soon discovered that the real world can be just as tiring as school, even more at times. I quickly became somewhat bored with real estate, and when my acceptance letter to med. school came the following spring, I thought I would go. But I was developing a nice real world routine which allowed me to focus on my spiritual journey. I stunned myself when I decided not to go, but something so much more important was on the line - Ultimate Truth.

I hooked up with a few good musicians, one of whom was heavily into mysticism as deeply and as seriously as I was. We developed a good friendship, but never really did much with our music. In my mind, even that was secondary to the spiritual progress toward going clear into cosmic consciousness. We tried organizing a direct marketing company, but it never got off the ground. I finally decided to do bio-medical research at Vanderbilt. This is something I was trained to do, and I could get back into a routine that would allow for my daily meditation excursions, without the financial worries of an unsteady income.

The following summer, I had another philosophy-shaking experience. I was driving in my

Granada early one evening on my way to see my brother and his wife, John and Carol. They have always been a great source of love and friendship to me, and I have always enjoyed getting together with them. As I crossed Highway 70 at Cross Timbers Road, a white Cadillac pulled out in front of me from the other side of Cross Timbers. I was forced to stop in the middle of the highway to let him go by. As I then tried to get on across the highway two teenage girls in another Granada came speeding over the rather blind hill on the highway. They struck me broadside at about 60 mph. As my car went into a full spin from the impact, I began reciting the 'lost word' of power and deliverance that I had learned from AMO. That lasted through the first 360 degrees and then I closed my eyes and said, "Dear God, please save me." My neck jerked back as the trunk of my car collided with a telephone pole. My right shoulder was bruised from the passenger side door which had collapsed all the way into the steering wheel. The telephone pole had crushed the car all the way through to the front seat. There was a tiny little area left in the cabin of the car where I was sitting, squished together from the collapsed metal on all sides. I managed to free my left arm to get to the doorknob and forced the door open. As soon as I stepped outside, I collapsed from the pain in my leg joint that meets with the pelvis (the acetabulum). I thought it might be fractured.

My brother's pastor had witnessed this whole drama and came down to see if I needed help. He had already phoned my brother who was on his way to the scene. I did not seem to be in any immediate danger, so the ambulance attendants let John drive me to the emergency room after I had signed some papers stating that I had refused their services. John could not even believe I was conscious when he saw the total destruction to my car. The doctor was surprised that I was in perfect shape without a drop of blood and all x-rays were negative. I was sore, but quite definitely free of serious injury. More than a few people including the doctor, nurses, and attendants considered this a miracle.

I was glad to be alive, but wondered if the lost word, the cry to God, or simple physics and luck had resulted in my survival. I didn't believe in luck, and the co-incidence of simple physics seemed a stretch. I was left with two alternatives. I did not want to stop or even slow down to think about that. I just wanted to move on and progress toward perfection. However, I found it more than curious that I had reverted back to calling on a personal God in an emergency as I had done in the sailing accident years earlier. I thought I must be more deeply brainwashed than I had ever realized. Was there any hope for me to escape the old pre-Aquarian way of thinking?

During this time, I met my first wife, Donna. Our first date was to a lecture on the golden age dawning on this planet. She was open to this optimism since her last few years had been rather difficult. Her ex-husband had been abusive, and this had resulted in her losing her first child 7 months into her pregnancy. She was still struggling with the fact that her father had left the family nearly 10 years earlier. She was ready for some joy, and my optimism about the Age of Aquarius was most appealing. We courted by letters since she spent the summer of 1977 in New Mexico, where her father was living. We moved in together that September after she came back to Nashville. I did not consider a marriage license anything necessary, since new age morality was a thing developed within each human heart. Such artificial boundaries of absolutes would not help in my spiritual progress, though I could see a functional place for them in society.

Donna found camaraderie with Nina, a member of the local AMO group, because both had been involved in white witchcraft. Nina was still quite active in her practice. She taught us about the power of femininity and how that was interrelated to the witch arts. The concept of the earth and the mother goddess Gaia opened my mind to a whole new way of approaching life. She also taught us the strength behind a constant state of gratitude. "Give all to the Divine Mother Force of the Universe," she would say. "Let every experience of life be seen as a gift from the Life force itself. When you see everything as a gift, you will claim nothing for yourself, and your attachments in this world will dwindle to none. Then you will be truly free to wield the power that only comes from not seeking any power." This reminded me of Chin's warrior heart. Yield to control. This paradox was an ever recurring theme in my quest.

We also met Dr. Outon in the local AMO group. He was a retired osteopath, so I was able to learn some healing arts from him. This gave me some gratification in light of my difficult decision not to go onto med. school. My whole purpose in going would have been to heal people anyway. By learning some osteopathy, acupressure, and homeopathy, I could still do that. I thought this would even be better, because I would be doing it as part of my religious quest, and not for the sake of taking money from sick people. He also introduced me to something that would give me a new hope for spiritual growth. He told me about a local metaphysical Unity church, whose members referred to themselves as truth students.

The first Sunday there was a new angle on truth searching for me. In Sunday School class, the members referred to Jesus as the Master and focused much of their discussion on the Bible. This was a fresh twist for me. I had always considered Jesus a great avatar, but had focused most of my efforts around a more eastern mysticism. The AMO was a western organization but its approach was still more like the mystery schools of Egypt and ancient Near East. This church was engaging in dialogue about more pragmatic aspects of living in the modern western world, and using the Bible as its manual for a successful mystical approach to life. Until that moment, I thought those particular scriptures were writings I might have to forsake forever, at least as far as any application to life is considered.

The aspect of Jesus as the greatest mystical teacher to have ever lived was also new. I learned that day that Christianity was the new mysticism that had taken all the great teachings of the world and delivered them through the Savior Jesus. But he was not the Savior because of a blood sacrifice on the cross, but because he was the first entity to return in the flesh without being bound to do so by karma. I did not understand this to be an 'official' line of the church, but it was expressed by most of the members. A small minority of them did not even believe in physical re-incarnation, but thought that we kept moving through different planes of existence from 'life-to-life' in a more spiritual way. I did not think that concept merited much and re-incarnation seemed more reasonable as most members believed.

This was also the first time I had ever witnessed any considerable degree of different opinions among truth disciples in matters concerning higher dimensions. The discussion that day was on the value of psychic experiences in our personal daily religion. As an AMO mystic, Dr. Outon defended the place of the psychic realm in our personal growth toward enlightenment. Claire, the lady leading the discussion, cautioned that it could interfere with our demonstration of success in this world, and that such success was an important evangelical tool to attract more people to the cause of the new era dawning upon the planet.

I shared some of my astral experiences with the class. I had to admit that nothing esoterically significant was ever learned during such excursions. I said, "I did enjoy them and had some confirmation of their realities, but had not been imparted any truths by such. However, the fact that such a dimension existed does assault materialism and agnosticism. There is a value there.

Furthermore, it is possible that some significant teaching could occur as skills develop on that level. I have just never gotten that far personally."

This is when I realized that the focus on Jesus and the Bible at Unity sort of replaced other aspects of new thought disciplines. Claire thought that all we needed to know about life and spiritual growth was to be found in the Bible, even though we had much to learn from the other great avatars who had lived through the ages. Her main point was that while other disciplines could help, Christian mysticism was enough to propel a person through to perfection and the godhead.

Most of the people there were into other things along with Unity, and I thought this new association was a great development in my life. I had longed for the church fellowship I had known while growing up. Now I had found the exact setting, only they were teaching metaphysical truths! Wow! Surely this was the missing element that would complete my disciplines and propel me into the next stage of personal and human evolution. Surely now the existential crisis I had created for myself was nearing a fulfilling and climactic resolution.

I had no idea that I was longing for this fellowship until I experienced it. Later that morning in chapel, a tear of joy came down my cheek as the congregation sang the Lord's Prayer during the worship service. Following that, the minister explained the true, mystical interpretation of the Lord's Prayer.

Our Father, = Divine creative Force of the Universe,

Who Art in heaven. = The storehouse of creative energy available to humans.

Hallowed be Thy name. = Our perfect selves are within us, set apart from the outer ignorant shell the Bible calls 'the flesh.'

Thy kingdom come. = May we enter the next stage of evolution on this planet.

Thy will be done. = May each of us perfect our own realities through mastering our thought and speech.

In earth = In the realm of this dimension we are trying to perfect

As it is in heaven = As in the realm where we realize we can manifest our storehouse of perfect creativity.

Give us this day our daily bread. = Let us now and forever realize our union with the perfect inner child within each of us. Let us never be anxious about anything brought about by ignorance of spiritual laws.

And forgive us our debts, = May we overcome our karma with enlightenment,

As we forgive our debtors. = As we are loving and forgiving to our fellow man in order to demonstrate that we are evolving to spiritual perfection.

And lead us not into temptation, = May we stay focused on our perfect divine nature,

But deliver us from evil. = Keep our minds on the truth and away from sin, which is ignorance of our divine nature and of the spiritual laws of the universe.

For thine is the kingdom, = Heaven is available now,

And the power, = And the power is yours to bring it forth.

And the glory forever = And can manifest in our lives forever from now.

He then did a meditation for the release of personal power within each of us. I was so high from the meditative state that I had achieved. His sermon was on the mystical meaning behind the sermon on the mount. He focused on the secret symbolism behind the images that fundamental Christians take literally. What I learned there brought the Bible in line with what I had come to believe from the eastern religious writings as well as the arcane teachings of the western mystics. I was now being made privy to the essence of all scripture ever written on behalf of progressing the human race to its next stage of evolution. I was thrilled that the Bible and Christian terminology fit into my belief system with the proper interpretation made privy from ascended masters:

Atonement means at-one-ment. When one becomes one with the universe and one with his perfect inner self, then atonement for ignorance of spiritual laws takes place.

Sin is ignorance. Ignorance results in sickness, poverty, and other evils of this world having power over me. I have nothing in the universe to fear.

Forgiveness is adding this knowledge and eliminating mortal thoughts from my consciousness. Forgiveness of sin is forgetting my old self and realizing my new higher self. When the God of the Bible says, 'I will remember your sins no more,' this is the figurative expression of this truth of canceling old karma by right thinking and affirmations.

God is good and God is everything. Therefore, evil in this universe is an   illusion. This illusion allusion reminded me of the Maya of Hinduism. Indeed, this was more confirmation that all religions ultimately proclaim the same basic truths. God is what anyone worships, because human worship is the worship of and from God, which is the sum total of everything. God, the

150

Father, is the Force as can be seen depicted in the Star Wars' movies.

The Christ of Greeks and the Messiah of the Hebrews and the Krishna of the Hindus are all one and the same in energy and consciousness. Each of us has within us this Christ consciousness, waiting dormant for us to negate our mortality and affirm our eternal divinity. I understood this was just another term for cosmic consciousness.

The Holy Spirit is the spirit of truth, just as the Bible says. But it is not a personal being of some Trinity. Rather, it is a principle of the Force of creativity and truth lying dormant within each one of us. This power is released as we negate our mortality and affirm our divinity, our Christ consciousness.

Born again is a term describing the act of bringing to the surface that perfect man that is dormant within each of us. The Divine Mind created each of us to be perfect, and when that perfection manifests, we are demonstrating that we are born again through mystical enlightenment.

The basic approach was to see the mind as a fertile garden or an active computer, capable of manifesting the divine power of creation. We learned to practice meditative affirmations and right thinking techniques. These methods were designed to change the circuitry of the mind into a positive mental attitude. Then, a positive reality would result, since our minds create the manifestation of our reality. We could thus achieve the greatest divine health, wealth, peace, and prosperity.

I was so hopeful that the spiritual emptiness that had crept into my life would be filled by the addition of a church setting to my array of other arcane disciplines. I also began an official relationship with a yoga organization for self-realization and another home study school similar to AMO. I was trying to balance a lot of disciplines in order to achieve the right combination for my most efficient path to enlightenment. Each one claimed to be all that was necessary for personal growth and development. I assumed they were right but I just could not get satisfied that I was doing all I could to grasp the ultimate truth of the universe. Other people that I would encounter in this new age jaunt all seemed to put together their own packages of disciplines that best suited their individual needs for growth and enlightenment. Nobody was practicing only one discipline. This fit well the religious theory that there are actually no absolutes, and no single path to the heaven of enlightenment.

I was taught that even such things as reincarnation were supported in the Bible. I never knew this before. One Sunday morning, I was happy to hear the teacher's response to a question from another member about whether or not Unity's doctrine supports re-incarnation.

The teacher answered, "Our focus is more on regeneration rather than death and/or re-incarnation. We are concerned that the new man through enlightenment will be born again into his next level of spiritual evolution. Therefore, we have no official position on re-incarnation. Nonetheless, there is biblical support for re-incarnation, and most members accept it as a necessary provision of a loving universe to give each man an opportunity to enter immortality through regeneration as demonstrated by the Master Jesus. In what is known as Peter's confession at Caesarea, Jesus asks his disciples who the people say that he is. You can find this dialogue in the sixteenth chapter of Matthew."

We all opened our Bibles to this passage. She then continued, "We will look at this passage, but it is also found in Mark 8 and Luke 9. Notice that the disciples give specific and general examples of who Jesus might be, and they are all figures of the past." She read the disciples' response as found in the sixteenth chapter of Matthew: 'Some say John the Baptist, others say Elijah, and others Jeremiah or one of the prophets.' Of course, Peter goes on to say that Jesus is the Messiah. This Messiah consciousness is the Christos of the Greeks or the Krishna of the Hindus. Even though Jesus was not any of those people, the important observation here is that this passage demonstrates that re-incarnation was a commonly accepted belief among Jesus' followers. He did not say, 'That is ridiculous. How could I come back as any of those people? That would be re-incarnation and we do not believe in re-incarnation.' He simply asked, 'But who do you say that I am?' Clearly, he did not correct them on the belief of re-incarnation. Another passage to look up is in the first chapter of John."

We all turned to the passage, and I was getting rather thrilled at this private, proper, mystical interpretation of the very book I thought would be a problem for my metaphysical viewpoint on life. This was great!

The teacher then continued, "Notice in verse twenty-one that the priests and Levites from Jerusalem ask John the Baptist if he is Elijah. It appears that these well educated representatives of their faith believed in re-incarnation and that this was the general consensus. Why else would they ask if John the Baptist could be someone who had obviously lived and died many years earlier?"

Then came the real clincher. The teacher

added, "Now let us look at one more passage. Look at the ninth chapter of John, since we are already in that book." Again, she paused as we all found this scripture. She then continued, "Here the disciples ask about the man born blind, whether he or his parents sinned, in past tense, to cause him to be born blind. Jesus says that in this case neither the man nor his parents sinned, but that the man was born blind in order that the works of God could be made manifest through him. Jesus did not correct the disciples' view that it was possible that this man had sinned before he was born, thus in a previous life. He just said that was not the case in this instance. Again, it is apparent that a general belief in re-incarnation was accepted by Jesus and among his contemporaries."

It appeared that my work and worship in Unity was fitting into my full plate of mystical foodstuffs just nicely. Donna was most interested in these groups and activities also, but complained about how boring yoga was. She also thought so many people who ran in these circles were just downright strange. We decided this was acceptable, however, because proper private interpretation of the Bible and other scriptures would not necessarily appeal to the mainstream of the world until the great shift in human evolution occurred. Besides, even though a few weirdo's inhabited these ethereal realms, one could not really say that the spiritual modernists had a monopoly on the most bizarre of the bizarre. This was especially true now that Punk and New Wave music and images were filling the screen from MTV, much of which Donna and I were thoroughly enjoying. Furthermore, some of the televangelists and telehealers working 'in the name of Jesus' were not what we thought were great role models.

She also liked the minister at our church as much as I did. He was a very loving man and to this day we hold a deep affection for one another. This body of people gave her comfort as well since she was initially raised a Mormon because her father leaned in that direction. There was a lot of emphasis on congregational fellowship in that group and she was happy to recapture a bit of that in a church setting such as Unity. Her mom was raised a Baptist and the Mormon church was not any help or comfort to her when they moved from New Mexico to Nashville. Unity was therefore a nice place for us to land since it fit in with our metaphysical beliefs and her background in the occult without any conflict in the basic belief systems. I quickly became active in the church, but that was interrupted by what would turn out to be a bizarre addition to my career portfolio.

Just as I was settling into my position as an

animal surgeon and physiology researcher at Vanderbilt, there was an interesting quirk presented into my life that came from the entertainment world. Steve Martin was holding a nationwide contest known as SMLAAASAC (the Steve Martin Look-Alike Act-Alike Sound-Alike Contest). I was a fan of his and several friends thought I captured his essence well when I would turn it on. They urged me to enter and I finally agreed to give it a try at the state-wide contest. I was a bit surprised when I won, and the next thing I knew, I was being flown to Atlanta for the regional contest.

The local press already picked up on this thing and I had promised on TV that I would cut my hair to Steve's style if I won the state-wide contest. As a creative artist, Donna developed a good technique for temporarily coloring my hair to match Steve's familiar silver, a technique which allowed me to wash it out after the performance. Also on TV, I promised that I would buy a new white suit if I won the regional contest. As things turned out, I got fitted for that new suit the day I returned from winning the regional contest in Atlanta. A week later, Donna and I flew out to LA for the grand finale at The Comedy Store on Sunset Strip. I still have the fish trophy that Steve handed me that night after I won the national finals. It was a lot of fun.

It was a most unusual dream-like state that

resulted from this time of my life. I never had any intention of doing comedy, but I would get calls at the lab to do commercials or conventions. Some rich daddy even hired me to show up at his daughter's birthday party as 'Steve.' The work from this finally got to be so much that I left the lab. I went on the road a few times, but mostly did one or two-night convention gigs, not your standard comedy circuit stuff.

It did not take long before I decided that I pretty much hated it the whole time. I was surprised at how seedy things could get in that business. I didn't enjoy the travel, especially since Donna did not always get to accompany me. Mostly, it was just that comedy as a career is not what I wanted to do. I liked music. I liked the lab. I thought about doing some kind of paranormal psychology or perhaps joining the ministry of Unity. But comedy was not my gig. I enjoyed meeting and working with the likes of Steve, Johnny Carson, Mike Douglas, Robin Williams, Billy Crystal, George Carlin, and Martin Mull, but comedy as a career just was not my bag.

The reason I bring all of this up is that while I was somewhat disappointed in the moral environment in which I so often found myself during this time, I was pleasantly surprised to see how many people in this industry were involved in mysticism as I was. To avoid tabloid mentality, I want to make it clear that I never witnessed 'immorality' or 'open mysticism' from the above mentioned larger name stars that I worked with. I never even saw most of them more than once. They were all gracious, brilliant, and scholarly during the few hours I spent with them. Those were actually the most pleasant moments of this brief career.

It was the people with whom I worked behind the scenes - limo drivers, managers, agents, travel connectors, entertainers 'on their way up,' and the like - with whom I would often engage in dialogue about religion and philosophy. Maybe it was southern California, maybe it was the industry, but nearly everybody had the latest groove on mystical enlightenment. That part of the scene was usually pretty cool, although a lot of phony-baloney hit me, too. I was a serious truth student, and didn't care to hear about the latest pop-mystico fad.

However, the prevalence of new age thought in the industry was most encouraging to me. Through the AMO and authors with arcane and theosophist influence, I knew that the time to evangelize the world with the mystical truth had come. I was learning that some degree of infiltration was necessary in order to start influencing the planetary consciousness toward being receptive to receive the new truths of the Age of Aquarius. Teachers, lawyers, politicians, and entertainers of all kinds were essential to this loose-knit unspoken conspiracy of new indoctrination. I wasn't always pleased about the air of secrecy surrounding this concept, but I accepted that it was necessary. People resist change, and the situation of new hope dawning on Spaceship Earth was no exception.

A few years before my brief glimpse into the comedy universe, I was thrilled when I first saw the movie 'Star Wars.' This represented to me the full-blown manifestation of this evangelicalism from Hollywood, the center of the entertainment world. This brought great hope to me. I was reminded of my brief encounter with Chin's spirit karate during the scene where Luke Skywalker defended against the practice beams with his eyes covered by the blast shield. Later, when I entered that same entertainment arena for a brief time, I was so excited to see this same basic belief system inundating all ranks of that influential industry.

However, on a personal level, as exciting and glamorous at times as my own flash of modest fame was, I went back to the lab after less than two years. I was stressed out from this industry as much as I appreciated its contributions to the new consciousness of the planet. As I mentioned, it wasn't for me. Besides, the work began to dry up anyway. The novelty of this contest only went so far, and I experienced first-hand the fleeting glory of that fickle business. It was getting pretty strange to drive around in limos in LA and come back to Nashville to pay my electric bill just in the nick of time before it got cut off.

That brief interval of traveling and entertainment mania was enough to put a strain on my relationship with Donna. Just as I had decided to go back to the lab, she decided that she wanted to call us quits. Fortunately, her departure from the marriage only lasted a few months. When she knew that my life was returning to a more normal pace without the entertainment world, she came back. We regrouped our lives and wanted to get back on the glory road to cosmic consciousness, though Donna was a bit more prone to enjoying a good party among friends every now and then. It annoyed her the way my quest for truth and enlightenment was often all-consuming.

While I was settling in a bit and recovering from the previous two years, I had a few counseling sessions with a minister from Unity. It was at that point that we began seriously considering whether I should go to Unity Village in Missouri to train for the ministry. It was decided that I would teach a few courses, and get a feel for the metaphysical pastorate. I was active in the Reagan campaign at the time, so we decided I would begin teaching after Christmas, following the presidential elections of 1980.

A spiritual struggle began as soon as this decision was made. For some unknown reason, my astral trips began turning into nightmares. My meditations were invaded by thoughts of failure and hopelessness. Then my regular sleep was disturbed. Images of Hollywood-like witches, demons, vampires, and monsters were becoming more common than I would care to admit. I discussed this only with Donna because I did not want word to get out that I was having spiritual difficulties if I was to consider the ministry. I understood that acceptance into Unity Village could be very strict in its requirements. What was this struggle all about? Were the cosmic masters testing my durability? Were there some mischievous entities just having a bit of fun? Were my psychic teachers with the AMO trying to communicate something to me? I was even disturbed that I was asking these questions. I just wanted a good night's rest. Again and again, that illusive peace for which I remained desperate was just out of reach. I took solace in the fact that I must be close to a big change toward perfection and these disturbances must be the birth pangs.

A few weeks after Christmas, I stopped my astral projection experiences. I had lost the psychic and mental energy required for such exercises. Fortunately, the bad dreams eased up a bit at that time. I began to do only short meditations, because invasions into them would begin after some period of time. This dried up the meditation problems. I started doing the AMO lessons every other week. Backing off from these participations seemed to ease the psychic craziness to a tolerable level. I wasn't losing my mind after all. How delightful.

Shortly after my twenty-seventh birthday, I taught my first course, called 'Working With Spiritual Laws.' As empty as I felt at times, perhaps I had come a long way from that terrifying Christmas ten years earlier. I delivered a lot of hope. I gave a lot of motivation. I pounded into the minds of my students over and over that the solution to any and all of their problems and difficulties was within their own perfect minds and hearts.

I taught, "God spoke the universe into existence. You can speak your own universe, your own reality, into existence. Guard your words carefully. They have the same creative power as God."

I could see on their faces despair and hope, grief and comfort, success and failure. I just knew that the choice was within each of their hearts. How I yearned to impart this reality to them, to set them free from their mortal bondage.

I continued to present my lessons in truth. I would teach, "You have nothing in this whole universe to fear. You are greater than any problem or solution that faces you. All circumstances with the appearance of negativity and evil are truly just opportunities for you to demonstrate the divine creative power within you. This is not fantasy. It is reality that you are writing your own script. If you don't like this movie, change it. You are the author. You are the actor. You are the director. You are the architect. You are the captain of your soul. You are the master of your fate. You are the creator of your own reality."

I affirmed this in my own consciousness, and felt pangs of hope and ecstasy during my lessons. But, ... how curious. So why then was the drive home after each lesson that I taught being accompanied by that nagging emptiness? There wasn't an answer to be found for that one. Were the students wrestling with these same misgivings? I felt so hypocritical. I would teach and exhort and encourage. Then I would collapse alone in my efforts toward divinity. Man, I was sick and tired of all this, and the heaviness was just too ridiculous. It was time to take charge once and for all.

Whatever it took, I would no longer be denied the peace and enlightenment for which I longed, and which I deserved. Either this stuff is the truth or not. If it is, I am going to demonstrate it in my life once and for all. I am going to 'know all' as that visitor to my bedroom ten years earlier had promised. I will conquer all of my ignorance. Enough. The consciousness of Christ will be mine!

It is probably obvious that I had some more things to work out before I was quite ready to train for the ministry at Unity. I thought I would be such a hypocrite to continue teaching others about achieving the greatest divine health, wealth, peace, and prosperity if I had not mastered this for myself. Furthermore, another tangent had also captivated the minds and hearts of Donna and me.

In some of our occult circles, we began to run across people who saw a socio-political and socio-economic counterpart to the paradigm shift that was soon coming to planet earth. In some ways, this was most disturbing. Apparently, just as I had been going through my own personal birth pangs before cosmic or Christ consciousness was to be mine, so was the entire planet preparing to go through birth pangs before the next jump in human evolution. This could mean social and economic upheaval.

Donna and I then investigated some suggested reading material talking about various world-wide conspiracies. Talk about some stuff that can weird a person out! We ran across different power-play propositions about groups such as the Trilateral Commission, Council on Foreign Relations, and various international commerce groups linked with communism. There were various 'patriot' organizations popping up around the country talking about illegal taxation in the US and an international banking conspiracy. The most disturbing thing about all of this was that much of it made sense; but, it was hard to distinguish truth from fiction and sensationalism from reality. There were also a lot of individuals just out to make a buck off of fear-mongering. Even more disturbing was how involved various bigotry groups were running in these same circles. Nonetheless, there were essential elements of truth to be found and that truth was disturbing in revealing the threat to the status of the U.S. as a free constitutional republic.

I wasn't even very excited about Reagan getting re-elected. What the conspiracy circles had taught was that the gap between the Democrats and the Republicans was not so wide when the trashing of the Constitution was considered. I thought Reagan was a likable guy, and a good motivater for self-reliance. I really liked him, but I did not work for his re-election campaign, or anyone's for that matter. I was blitzed by this new data about the threat to our constitutional republic, and I hadn't noticed any radical change toward preserving it under Reagan's first administration. I contrasted this with my thrill of the 1980 elections, and this made me rather sad. I just had to let it go with, "Oh well, the truth is not always an easy thing to digest."

What was really odd was that we found ourselves associating with Christians, and they were the most sensible people in their approach to American history and the current problems both nation-wide and world-wide. It was the Christians who thought the bigotry groups and new agers in these anti-conspiracy movements were nuts, and they were quite right. The bigotry groups were trying to convince the Christians that they had a biblical basis for their positions of hatred and prejudice. It was the Christians who had the courage to stand up to their hatred and boldly declare that racism was anything but biblical. The new agers were trying to ignore the Christians and focus on the coming paradigm shift, and how each mystic must prepare for the coming socio-economic collapse. Many of the Christians in these circles said that indeed a change was coming, and there would be birth pangs, but that they would be followed by the second coming of Jesus. Meanwhile, the hard-core survivalists ranged from atheist to occult practitioners to so-called Christian identity freaks, and all focused mostly on the historical cycle of fallen empires, and said that the time for the collapse of the United States was near. Everybody saw imminent upheaval, but they all had different reasons and scenarios. It was chaos blended with truth, a most deadly and confusing combination! Panic was the prescription they were selling. Each was competing for the money and attention of anyone who would listen to their rhetoric.

There were two things that were most distressing about all of this. First, there was an element of truth to what was being spoken. Second, it was sad that the points of agreement were outshined by the points of dissension, which were huge. I mean to tell you - Christians and new agers, bigots and peace-lovers, fear-mongers and rational thinkers, money-lovers and true freedom lovers. Most of these people seemed to lack an anchor in their lives. Like I said, it was nuts, but it appeared that so much to be learned about problems in America was available if it could be weeded out of the insanity, hatred, and ignorance. It is still so sad that the right information from all of this has been lost because it has become identified with so much that is crazy, hateful, and on the fringes of reason at best. This is the closest I believe I was ever exposed to cult-like thinking.

Donna and I finally decided to do what seemed most reasonable in light of this confusion - leave the city. In the silence of simplistic whole-earth country living, we could clear our minds and hearts and get to the essence of what was important by living with only the basic necessities of life. I still remember what she said shortly before our decision. "If it is one room with a dirt floor, that would be fine with me. I just want to rid my mind and heart of all the unnecessary clutter of this world. I want to live so basic that the only thing I can experience is purity, whatever I may ultimately discover that to be. I just want to see and know one pure thing before I die."

We did determine that what most of these anti-conspiracy circles had in common was that the cities were to be less and less inhabitable in the future years. At the very least, it seemed sensible to have a country place available for recreation, if not a future necessity for decent living or even survival. Ideally, we could eventually have a haven prepared in the country, and live in the city for convenience. We agreed with another fellow that we would move to a farm about 35 miles out of Nashville, and set up the haven. In the spring of 1985, we started working on a rough structure for shelter. That would eventually go to our partner after we built another main structure for the whole farm, which is also where Donna and I would live, and perhaps eventually have kids. We actually closed the deal in July and moved in August.

Donna and I thought we would probably move back into the city after the farm was set up and paid off with the aggressive mortgage we had set up with the owner. This was to take only two years, but our partner quickly grew tired of the new difficult lifestyle. We were living in what would probably technically be classified as sub-poverty, though the simplicity of the lifestyle had certain appeals, in a third-world kind of way. We were building housing and putting in plumbing gradually as we lived out there, so life was most difficult at first. After less than two month's, our partner's trust and spirit collapsed and he ran back to the comfort of the city with that month's mortgage money in his pocket. Timetables obviously changed.

This was turning into more difficulty than we had originally planned. I was starting to feel way off course from my spiritual search. The first year was very challenging indeed. We had structured everything to include a partner, and his abandonment of the project had really thrown us off course. That first winter was very cold, especially since the insulation was hardly adequate to keep in the heat generated from our modest woodstove.

There was not yet indoor plumbing. However, the novelty of this experience was quite delightful, and a good survival routine was developed.

I developed a nice sense of unity with my surroundings early every morning as I would split wood and crank up the stove before driving into Vanderbilt. I was working four 10-hour days which gave me a three day weekend at the farm to cut and split wood for the coming week. I would also store up water for bathing and dishwashing, etc. Our well was tapped into a sulfur water table, so we would fill jugs and let them air out for our drinking water. I hoped that all of this hard-living survivalist experience would strip me of the clutter and confusion of my last 12 years of nirvana-searching. I was hoping the essence of only the truth would be all that remained.

Things got a bit easier after a year. I could go out onto the deck of our half-finished country house, and star-gaze myself tantalizingly close to a familiar, peaceful place in my mind and heart. I knew it was a place that I had once felt as a toddler in Texas, but I could not quite embrace the simple peace that rises above all thought and feeling. Looking up into that vast sky would give me the reassurance that somehow everything made sense, and I could someday, hopefully soon, grasp the sense of it. It was still eluding my efforts and I was tiring of the struggle. But I was trapped. I could not rest until I knew what I had to know about the essential truth of all that is, whatever that could be. Yet I needed rest from this weary war which was wayward. Wow! What woeful alliteration.

It was November, 1986. A nice warm mid-Tennessee night that can often be felt fighting off the impending cold of winter that is nonetheless inevitable. That's the way November is there. It's always nice to be reminded, even before winter starts, that spring will come soon. These weather observations are even more significant when you are living a basic life away from comfort control by a switch on the wall. I joined Donna on the deck to take advantage of the temperature which would become less and less familiar as December and then January approached. Usually the clear nights resulted from humidity being blown out by heavy dry northern air, so it was unusual to have such a clear night in November when the temperature was also warm.

I quietly sat down on a big cable spool the telephone men had left behind. It made a neat table and chair in this setting. I looked up and found Orion, Pleides, and the Big Dipper. They were nice familiar constants to that big sky full of supernovas and redshifting expansion. I then asked, "Donna, a few months before we moved out here, you said something about simple living and just experiencing something pure. Do you remember that? It sounds almost stupid, but, uh, have you gotten even close to knowing what that purity is?"

"Mark, before we get started on this, I want you to just listen for a while. Okay?" I nodded and smiled, rolling my eyes as if to understand my impatient nature when it came to the subject of enlightenment and self-mastery.

Donna continued, "Now let's consider this purity, or peace, or essence of life, or whatever you want to call it. Maybe it's really simple, and the trick is to accept that it is really simple. Maybe it's just this moment, or a moment like this one. We have enough food, and our bodies are fed. It is a beautiful evening. The night bugs sound great, and that crescent moon is beautiful. I understand you want to know where it all came from and what it all means, but perhaps just accepting it and being thankful for this nice moment is what it all means. I know, I know, you want to ask, 'Thankful to who or what?' Listen, I don't know, but maybe I just don't need to know. Maybe you don't need to know. Just relax, take a deep breath and enjoy that sky, and this beautiful land around you and this neat house you have built with your own hands. One that you are continuing to finish, I remind you. If there is something or someone greater than you who wants you to know more about it all, then you will just have to accept their timetable. You are going to drive yourself mad with desperation. You know the classic simple philosophy of the mystics. 'Be here now.' You know it, but you have such trouble practicing it. With all the yoga and meditation you do, that much you should have learned. You have probably read every book in the universe on mysticism and cosmic enlightenment. If anyone has a textbook understanding of the path to divinity, it is you. You need to accept that there is nothing you have missed. No author. No organization. No technique. No religion. No philosophy. I think your persistence, diligence, even obsession over these years is commendable, but you are going to go crazy searching for something that may not be in your control to find and have. Man, is there possibly anything more you could do other than practice more the art of acceptance? I'll tell you the answer. It is no." She looked at me with that look of 'Hmmm? Do you get it?'

I furled my brow with a look of exasperation with myself, smiling with humorous self-abasement. "I know what you're saying, but you were the one who wanted to see the one pure thing. But, well, okay Donna. You're right. I don't need to talk about it. I don't need to read anymore. I don't need to chant affirmations or visualize any kind of realities into existence. We have a pretty neat life out here, albeit difficult for now. I just need to perform the tasks at hand. And when I meditate, I will just see myself at peace and knowing all in the bliss of cosmic consciousness. The lilies and the sparrows do not toil or fret. Neither should I. I am just going to hold to that picture of myself. At peace and enlightened. That should attract what I want and need. That's the reality I must create. I'll just keep the image simple. If it takes a lifetime or more, well then, so be it. I need rest from this search. I just need some rest."

I did sleep well that night. And for a couple of weeks, I was really at peace. I actually experienced some absolute rest, almost a vacation from the quest. It was a good thing, too, because I was about to be engaged in the greatest spiritual battle of my life.

Chapter 6

Survival, Revival,
and Times Square

The Sunday after our little discussion on the deck, I was completing a three day fast. Water only. I would cup my hands around the glass and meditate upon radiating power into the water. I would visualize the wisdom energy of the Universe pouring into the liquid. Then I would drink this water of light with ecstatic gratitude. I thought such a fast would solidify my self-vow to accept my lot and affirm the visualization of simple peace and enlightenment, without any other complications. This fast provided a feeling of self-control, discipline, and thus a control of reality. I sat in the lotus, eyes turned upward focusing on the third eye. I held to the image of myself at peace and fully enlightened. I affirmed that the hunger in my belly did not matter and neither did the starvation in my soul. A simple self-fulfilling formula was generated. I convinced myself that denying any power the feeling of emptiness held over my joy would actually fill some of the void.

It was reminiscent of the instructions from our friend Nina - "Claim nothing for yourself, and your attachments in this world will dwindle to none. Then you will be truly free to wield the power that only comes from not seeking any power." Releasing attachments to this world must also include letting go of personal desires of the heart for the knowledge of pure truth. Was this the ultimate in witchcraft? Forget spells and manipulation of reality. Perhaps I must live a mystical paradox. What about giving up the desire to comprehend any ultimate reality as the means of actually attaining that enlightenment? This reasoning was along the same lines as Chin's warrior heart - "Yield to control." Unity's favorite saying was 'Let go and let God.' This applied here. Also relevant were the words of the guru at the kundalini ashram - "A man who can sit still does impress me." He must have been referring more to a stillness of the mind as well as that of the body. Had it finally sunk into my thick skull? Could I embrace the famous words of Desiderata? - "No doubt the Universe is unfolding as it should." Could I believe those words applied to me also? I was beginning to think I could answer 'Yes' and just knew my goal was near now that I was no longer seeking it. This was indeed unfolding as a mystical paradox. Knowing the unknowable meant not trying to know it. (And some people say that certain aspects of mysticism are confusing).

After a couple of weeks, even tough and observant Donna made a comment with her all too familiar hint of sarcasm. "Mark, I have got to say that you have been remarkably easy as of late. I honestly think you are getting a grip on this enlightened consciousness thing. It is quite a relief."

"Donna, I'm telling you I really do feel better. You helped you know. I mean, I know I have heard it a thousand times but it is true to just 'Be here now' and 'Let go and let God' and 'Yield to control' and however many ways there are of saying, 'Hey, cool it right where you are. You have what you need, and you will get what you need when you need it, and that includes cosmic consciousness and eternal peace.'"

She responded, "Great, now make sure there is plenty of wood split before you go into the lab. I know you wanted to go in a bit early today since the new people are arriving."

In other words, she was done talking about it and ready to move on with the survival necessities. This was not a cold or insensitive response to my statements, just a stark reminder of the realities of what it took to get by considering how we lived. The first real taste of winter was moving in that day and she did not want to get caught without enough wood for the stove, since that was our only source of heat. We had a backup kerosene heater, but the man who refills the kerosene tank had not come out to visit us yet. Furthermore, I usually got home late these days since I was going in after lunch and staying well past supper. This might be especially true since there were new people coming into the lab today and this might add a little more work time than the usual.

"Okay. Okay, " I said lightly as I grabbed the splitting ax.

As I was going out the door, she stopped me and put her hands on my shoulders. With gentle sincerity, she said, "Hey, I did not mean to cut you off. I am really glad that this nirvana quest is at a better place for you." We both smiled with the humor of her term 'nirvana quest.' She gave me a hug and added, "I know you work so hard out here and at the lab, and I know your spiritual search means a lot to you. I respect all of that, Mark. I hope you know that. And I really am glad you are happy with where things are for you right now. I just don't want it to drive you crazy. A little peace fits you well. I like it. I really am glad for you. I hope it lasts."

"Thanks," I said. "Uh, thank-you. I'm sorry I get kinda crazy with it, but I think I'm almost there. If only." Then I smiled, "Just kidding."

We laughed at that and I went on out to split the day's wood. I think she knew my peace would not last long. It never had before. She respected that I sought this pearl of wisdom, whatever it may be, but she knew I was probably just on vacation before the next onslaught. Of course she was right. Things were already changing as I returned to the farm that evening about 11:00. After my solid peaceful meditations for enlightenment, my efforts were already being thwarted. I couldn't believe what I encountered at the lab that day. I was exasperated at what I must now tolerate. How could this be? The new people in the lab were ... Christians! Argh!

It seemed like they were now coming out of the woodwork from every direction in my life. I had become very good friends with Stan, a local talk show host who was very well read on any and all the latest information concerning various threats to the US Constitution. He was intelligent, as passionate about America as I was, and very likable. The problem was that he was serious about his Bible-believing Christian faith. Nonetheless, our friendship blossomed. Donna also thought he was a really nice guy, but she hated that he was a Christian even more than I did. He had great kids also who were around our age. They were wonderful people, but were all Christians. It was most irritating because we really enjoyed their company. Their faith was tolerable because we only saw them once or twice a week.

But now I had to put up with it at the lab as well. The two new ladies, Ginny and Liz, were also around the age of Donna and me. They were bright and were also well aware of threats to the freedoms in America. They were puzzled that I was so well-informed on these subjects, knew a considerable amount of the Bible, and was yet a new-age truth searcher. Like so many Christian authors had purported , they believed the new age was just another facet to the assault on America's greatness and its Christian heritage.

First I came with the over-used line, "Oh, you mean the Christian heritage that founded a nation where slavery was legal and women couldn't vote under the new Constitution for over a century." It was a cheap shot. I knew enough history to know that Christianity had actually played a major role in eliminating slavery, even though some hypocrites had used the Old Testament as a phony justification supporting this grotesque practice. They were quick to point this out to me. I also knew that there were Christian leaders who had supported women's suffrage. My Pop Moerner was such a young man long before I was a twinkle in my dad's eye.

Then I moved on and hit them with one of Jesus' line from the Sermon on the Mount. "Ladies," I said, "didn't Jesus say 'Be ye perfect as your Father in Heaven'? Now that doesn't seem to fit your view that we are all imperfect sinners without a chance of correcting ourselves. Why would Jesus give us a command that he knew we could not keep? He told us to be perfect, and that is exactly what I am striving to be, or at least to become. Granted, I have not made it yet, but I will. We all will. Why else would Jesus give us that command? Do you intend to obey that command and become perfect, or do you intend to give up and say you are just a lost sinner, and someone else will have to do the work for you?"

At first, it appeared they were a bit shocked at their new workmate. I was almost viscous, certainly pompous; but I meant well, and stood by what I believed with integrity. Ginny responded, "Yes, Mark, we are commanded to be perfect, but we also believe we are incapable by our own power of keeping that command. The only way to please God is through faith by the power of the Holy Spirit. The only way to have that power is through the cross of Jesus."

I was irritated, but this was their first day, and we were all nice people. I did not want to get into a heavy discussion that might start us off on the wrong foot. After a bit more exchange, I simply said, "Fair enough." I left it at that, and they did not push. Enough had already transpired that I felt burdened by all of this.

Donna found a rather battle-weary husband returning home from work that night. As I walked in the door, the lentil soup smelled really great. Donna was listening to a tape Stan had loaned us about how international banking had influenced FDR and Congress to go off the gold standard, but that would require another book. When Donna saw me, she immediately said, "Man, work or something was tough today. How 'bout some soup?"

"Yes, thank-you. That sounds good," I answered as I gave her a hello kiss. She sat there listening to the tape, indicating that I could get the soup myself, which I did.

I put another log in the woodstove and then got a nice bowlful with some herbal tea. As I sat down, Donna stopped the tape and said, "Okay, what's going on? I can see struggle written all over your face. Are the new people jerks or something?"

"No, no, they are really nice. I mean, they

are really great people. They're just, you're not going to believe this. They're just ... Christians. Real ones. Like Stan. They know all about the latest conspiracy theories and even have quite a handle on what's fanatical nonsense and what is pretty real and relevant. They think it's neat what we are setting up out here. It's a couple of ladies about our age.

"Do they have names?" Donna asked.

"Oh yes. Uh, Ginny and Liz"

"Are they pretty?" was her next question.

Now Donna could be known to have a jealous streak, though she was quite secure with her femininity. Nonetheless, I kept her green eyes in mind when I responded to that question. I answered, "They are not ugly."

"You mean they're beautiful?"

"No, I mean they are not ugly. Listen, Donna, they are Christians. You know, the enemy?"

What I meant by that was Christians are the main groups holding up the evolution of the planet. I was relatively tolerant compared to some of our occult friends who were quite radical in their animosity toward Christianity. Believing in somebody else's work for 'salvation' was a definite mountain in the middle of the planet's path to Aquarian freedom. And that is just what Christians believed. That somebody had died 2000 years ago and that made everything okay. Talk about a cop-out.

Along with other metaphysicians, mystics, and truth students, I was willing to take responsibility for my own place in the universe. It seemed so odd that these Christians I encountered in conservative political circles could talk of personal initiative and personal responsibility as far as politics and life in America, but when it came to eternal matters, somebody else was responsible for your well-being. They hated Big-Daddy government, but they embraced a Big-Daddy Jesus who rendered them free of responsibility for their 'sins,' what I knew of course as karma and ignorance. It just seemed so irreconcilable, but Stan and now my new associates at the lab were persistent that their positions were rational.

So Donna understood she had nothing of which to be jealous. In fact, as time went on, she ended up developing a good friendship with Ginny and Liz. However, she was not initially too pleased with them for loaning me tapes on Christian apologetics. Between Thanksgiving and Christmas, I must have listened to more than 20 hours of their propaganda. From our farm, I had a nearly one-hour drive each direction to and from work every day, four times a week. I passed that drive time listening to tapes, be it music, organic farming, survival skills and self-sufficiency, politics, even comedy.

Now it was Christian apologetics. Arming myself with their data in order to shoot it down. Associating daily with Christians was getting to be a real hassle. A new doctor I was to work with came on the scene, and, you guessed it, this guy was a Christian. What a pain in the neck. So I thought once and for all, I would put an end to their assault. I thought the best way would be to hear their arguments with an open mind, thus demonstrating they should do the same for me. I wasn't quite ready to read the Bible front to cover. I couldn't think of a bigger waste of time, but I was willing to hear some of their tapes. I had to admit that a lot of what I heard was new material. I had never encountered anything quite like this. These tapes weren't the basic heaven and hell and sins and the cross kind of stuff, although that message was included. This was different. There were some ministers, but also scientists, doctors, lawyers, economists, philosophers, even former mystics, which really baffled me. I wondered how anyone so serious about the truth could have fallen back into mechanistic, out-dated, pre-Aquarian Christianity. But I was priding myself as having an open mind, and I had once again become so desperate for the truth that I was willing to put up with even this if it was somehow a necessary step toward enlightenment.

One night, I seemed to get a warning against this material. I was deep in meditation. I was startled to see a clear image before me of what I assumed was the face of an ascended master. His smile seemed kind enough, but there was something mysterious about his countenance. Honestly, more than mysterious. It was as if he was hiding something from me. Something about who or what he was. I ignored the almost ritualistic fear that came with his presence. If he was hiding something, I thought it must be for my own good. So that I could discover it for myself, perhaps. The image spoke. It was absolutely amazing the way my mind clearly heard his message. He said, "Caution your present direction. Follow my way. Be not led astray. Stay on course." Was I losing some of the ground I had gained in my spiritual evolution by over-exposing myself to devolved Christian information? Was he telling me to avoid what these Christians had to say?

I had to admit that by Christmas, I had become more than disturbed by some of the information imparted to me by those tapes. I surprised myself by listening several times to the 'testimony' of a former mystic, Dr. Gold, who had some interesting things to say about the Bible. He was actually born a Jew and rejected that faith in search for metaphysical realities with a journey quite similar to my own. This was disturbing, but I was certainly going to make sure my questful adventure did not conclude like his. I was not to become an ignorant fundy after all the effort I had put forth in an attempt to seize ultimate reality. However, this guy was no idiot, and had covered much of the same ground I had. I was somewhat impressed and curious. So, I listened.

First of all, he brought up a very interesting point about reconciling one's personal philosophy with the Bible. I had to admit that I had pondered this before. I eventually abandoned this question for lack of progress toward an answer. But now it was addressed in such a way that I could no longer ignore it. 'Why were all of these mystic philosophies trying to reconcile their teachings with the Bible?' The Christians were not trying to reconcile their religion with other religious and philosophical writings. They were content to accept the Bible and reject others that contradicted it. So why couldn't I and other truth students just reject the Bible, rather than force it to fit what we believed? I had always assumed the answer was that we mystics believed there was truth in all religions and the Bible must be included there. But this particular philosopher made me face a tough reality. The reality of common sense.

I had to finally admit that the Bible was pretty clear about its basics. And those basics were not mysticism. I was sickened at the thought of what they were, so I had to reject the basics of the Bible. This made my experiences at Unity Church seem rather ridiculous and phony. It had been a sort of cut-and-paste approach to the Bible. I guess the first scripture to go would have to be 2 Timothy 3:16. Not good scholarship and not good religion. Regarding the Bible and my mysticism, I had just been plain dishonest. It was not easy to hear information that made me face this.

Nonetheless, I forced myself to listen and admit what the Bible clearly taught. After all, I did not fear that I would be led astray from my goal. I winced courageously, knowing I must reject the following biblical summary: (1) There was One God as three distinct persons, Father, Son, and Holy Ghost. (2) Only Jesus, the only begotten Son, was God in the flesh. (3) He died on the cross for a reason, not just for the fun of it, and that reason was to reconcile a chaotic, sinful universe back to an infinite personal Creator. (4) Man seemed to be at the core reason for this rebellious chaos. (5) Man was incapable of reconciling himself back to this Creator. That last one was the clincher. I had long since rejected that position big-time. Dr. Gold was convinced that no reading

of the Bible could fairly and justifiably be inter-
preted that it said anything else other than salvation through the cross of Jesus. He gave numerous citations.

The third chapter of John contains the most
famous, of course. "Just as Moses lifted up the
serpent in the desert, so the Son of Man must be
lifted up, that everyone who believes in him may
have eternal life. For God so loved the world that
he gave his only begotten Son, that whosoever believes in him shall not perish but have eternal life.
For God did not send his Son into the world to con-
demn the world, but to save the world through him.
Whoever believes in him is not condemned, but
whoever does not believe in him stands condemned
already because he has not believed in the name of
God's one and only Son."

Included also were the third, eighth, and
fourteenth chapters of John, and the second, third,
fourth and ninth chapters of Romans. The list went
on and on with the second and third chapters of
Galatians, the fourth chapter of Acts and so many
verses. There were even many Old Testament
citations such as the sixty-fourth chapter of Isaiah
and all of the prophetic visions found in the fifty-
third chapter. I am able to write these down now
because I recorded them from his interview and
looked them up. Obviously, I kept those notes. The

only way to reconcile all of these citations as symbolic of a mystical pantheistic view of life was to read the text with ignorant biased presupposition to a far greater degree than what I had accused the Christians of doing. An objective, open mind could only reach one conclusion, but because the conclusion was unacceptable, reconciliation through figurative symbolic rewriting had to take place. I was being forced to admit that such reconciliation was not logical. Yet I wanted to be logical and open minded in my rational thought. Reconciling mysticism and the Bible was dishonest, phony, and unacceptable scholarship. This was a terrible dilemma.

Dr. Gold even addressed the very scriptures I thought supported re-incarnation. His knowledge of Jesus' contemporary Judaism was impressive, and he relied upon this in his explanations. First came the understanding of the spirit of prophets. The whole history of the idea of the Holy Spirit was rooted in the spirit of God. He explained how the Holy Spirit dwelled in the Holy of Holies in the Old Testament and then came forth as the Comforter when the curtain was torn in the temple, as described in the twenty-seventh chapter of Matthew and the fifteenth chapter of Mark. This same concept was all that the evangelists meant when they wrote of the question to John the Baptist, "Are you Elijah? Are you that prophet?" The interrogators were only asking if the same 'spirit' that had come upon Elijah was the one that was now upon John. I was a bit angered at the pathetic academia of metaphysics that had led me to the conclusion that this scripture supported re-incarnation. The same was true when Jesus asked the disciples who the people said he was, and they answered Elijah, John the Baptist, or one of the prophets. They were not saying that the people believed Jesus himself had actually lived as one of these people. They were saying that the spirit that made them prophets was also the same spirit that gave Jesus his power. The scripture of the man born blind was explainable that the disciples were aware of a common discussion among rabbis of their time that a child could have sinned in the womb. Even more likely was the idea of the sins of the father being visited upon the child as seen in the twentieth chapter of Exodus or the fifth chapter of Deuteronomy. This is what I mean that Jesus' contemporary Judaism was historically considered and applied in Dr. Gold's scholarly approach. Clearly, re-incarnation was not intimated, and I had to admit that it was almost a bold-faced lie to use these scriptures to support re-incarnation. To use terminology from the deep south, it was down-right embarrassing.

Now I was forced to question my faith in my previous teachers in all areas of metaphysical education. What was already clear was that the Bible had to be rejected if I was to embrace mysticism. That was the only reasonable and honest conclusion. I would do that if necessary, but I had never considered it necessary before. The arguments that the Bible had been changed and that re-incarnation had been eliminated turned out to be absurd. I was ashamed at my readiness to accept what someone such as Shirley Maclaine had to say about such matters when their positions were completely untenable with good scholarship. I could no longer say Jesus was just a great teacher, or a good man, or just another avatar. The gospel accounts had not twisted his words. The Bible clearly and accurately recorded his teachings. I had to say he was an egomaniacal jerk if I was to reject his obvious message of salvation. To be honest, I was beginning to panic. It was disconcerting to admit that a good mystic had to personally reject Jesus if he was to reject fundamental Christianity. What a drag! I could no longer fake this issue out of consideration in my own personal philosophy. I had to choose.

Dr. Gold continued as he spoke of the first time he ever read the third chapter of Genesis. This is also a familiar passage to many people. It is when the narrative character Satan, disguised as a serpent, tempts Eve when he says, "You will not surely die. For God knows that when you eat of the forbidden fruit your eyes will be opened, and you will be like God, knowing good and evil." For the first time, this passage hit me hard and in a new way. 'You will be as gods.' I knew that was exactly what I was trying to do. If that serpent was right, then he was the good guy, and the God of the Bible was some self-absorbed bully on this universal block. But that did not gel with the rest of the biblical picture. I mean, get real, a bully God who comes in the flesh and dies for mankind? I don't think so! Again, here was another example that I couldn't reconcile my own philosophy with that of the Bible. What a pain this all was, but I could no longer ignore it out of fear. I would now face this challenge with courage and rational resolve to know the truth.

Such self-proclaimed courage did not prevent the fact that I began to toss and turn in my sleep like never before. Here came the monsters again. What if it really was as clear-cut as my Christian friends said it was? What if I was simply a man, a mortal, destined to live only once and then to enter an eternity based upon a simple decision regarding Jesus. The image of an eternal darkness devoid of the presence of God, of love, took my breath away. I snapped out of it. "No way. That's ridiculous and absurd. How dare such thoughts invade my mental territory!" I was ready for the two weeks I had scheduled to take off for Christmas break.

On my night rides back to the farm, if I wasn't listening to tapes, I enjoyed flipping through the various talk shows on AM-Radio. On the drive home from my last day at work before the break, I tuned into a moderator who was taking calls about the meaning of Christmas. He then announced he was going to tell a Christmas story. I cleared the static up a bit and settled in for the remainder of the journey. I had just passed the Lebanon exit, which meant I was almost home. The radio host began his story:

"There was once a nice American family in a nice American farm home located in a nice American town in a lovely valley. The lovely wife and her three lovely children were getting ready to go to a special Christmas Eve Church service. They were excited but also a little sad. The husband did not believe in God, and certainly thought the whole Christmas story was just a nice legendary myth. As the wife pleaded one last time for the husband to join them, he responded with his usual animosity toward the whole affair. He was a nice enough man, but he said, 'Dear, you know how I feel about the Jesus story. I mean, really, God coming in the flesh? If there was a God, why would he bother coming to earth as a man? It just doesn't make sense. I love you and the kids, and I think it is fine for you to worship the way you want, but you know I do not want you trying to drag me into all of this. Now have a good time. Good-bye, kids. I love you. Bye, bye.' It began to spit snow as the family was pulling out of the driveway. A nice snow storm was predicted. He checked his bird-houses to make sure there was plenty of food be-cause he loved the hundreds of different birds that depended upon him, especially through the win-ter. They lived just next to the barn.

"After a couple of hours, the storm began to really pick up. His wife called to say they would stay at the church until it cleared up and that they might even come back in the morning. They had a good four-wheel drive, so he knew they would make it just fine even if it meant driving through a foot of snow the next day. But another problem occurred. Suddenly the birds he loved and cared for began banging into his window. The wind and snow had become so furious that they could not find their housing he had built for them. They were crashing into the window by the dozens and hun-dreds! He knew he must do something to help.

"He then realized he could open up the barn

door and let them stay in there for the night until the blizzard was over. He bundled up and fought the wind outside until he opened up the barn door. He turned the inside light on so the birds would see it, but they just kept banging into the window of the house. He went back near the window and tried to get their attention to herd them over to the barn, waving and flapping his arms. But the birds kept trying to go into the window. He knew they would perish if he didn't do something, but he was desperately out of ideas. In anguish, he cried out, 'If only I could become one of them long enough to show them the way to safety.' He paused, and the wind and snow immediately began to lighten enough for the birds to make their way into the barn for the night. The man thought again about what he had just said. 'If only I could become one of them long enough to show them the way to safety.' The truth of the incarnation of Jesus hit him forcefully and knocked him to his knees. At that moment church bells began ringing from town and throughout the valley. He wept and prayed and celebrated Christmas like never before. For the first time, he was celebrating the birth of the only begotten Son of God."

I reached over and turned off the radio. For a brief moment, I was frozen. I resisted the urge to allow this story to move me. Then, something odd happened (as if the rest of this is normal). An image of Jesus in a khaki-colored robe came to my mind for a few seconds. It was odd, because I saw him sitting on a rock by a river, and he was simply thinking about me. He turned to me and smiled gently, and the image disappeared from my mind. My eyes watered up, but I caught myself. I spoke out loud, almost in anger, "Man, what is going on? This is stupid!" I took a deep breath and continued talking to myself. I blew out the breath continuing, "Whew. Okay, let's just keep it together now. Alrighty. Everything's cool. No problem." I had reached the road to the farm by now. "Good, good. I'm nearly home and my Christmas vacation has begun. Okay. Great." I was just pulling into the farm's quarter mile long driveway.

After I went into the house, I settled into the thrill of two weeks off. I then told Donna the story I had heard on the radio. When I came to the part about what the man said about becoming one of the lost birds, I became a bit emotional. This was not conducive to a pleasant scene, but I couldn't help myself. I finally got through the story. Donna was staring at me with her head slightly tilted down and an expression of disgust.

Her look matched her words as she said, "Oh, brother, you're turning into a fundamentalist. Could you at least put it off until after the holidays, so they are not ruined!"

I replied, "No, Donna, I am not becoming a fundy. Surely you know that. It just seemed like a nice story. You know. Well told. I have always been a sucker for that. How many people do you know get teary-eyed at a bad movie if the musical score is still good? This radio tale was no different. I don't really believe it. Christmas is just an emotional time. Don't take it as a big deal. I'm just struggling a bit with a few of the things we have always believed, that's all."

"You mean like re-incarnation and the Bible? You're not going to get started on that again, are you?"

"No, I'm just ... trying to figure a few things out. Shouldn't we be able to hear all sides? I'm not going to become a fundy just because some of what they say might make sense."

"Mark, listen. I will be as gentle about this as possible." She paused, and then said, "Well, you're kinda freaking me out with all this Christian junk. Now, please just stop listening to that propaganda for a while. It's really scary. I love you. I don't want to lose you to this stuff. You're getting like a cult mentality."

"I am not, Donna. C'mon. I'm a scientist. I know how to do research, and I am just giving a fair hearing to all sides, so I can reach a rational conclusion. You know how that works. Look, I am not going to become a Christian. You of all people should know that. They just might have some information to offer, so I could tie up some loose ends about what I know and believe. That's all." I spoke with reserve and playful bravado as I stuck my chest out, feigning a deep voice, "I'm not leaning toward Bible-believing Christianity."

She smiled and said, "Well, you better not. It goes without saying that I will be gone if you do. I wish those people would just leave you alone, and that you would quit reading their books and listening to their tapes."

I responded, "Hey, it's not like I'm absorbed with it or anything."

She interrupted, "You get absorbed with everything you do."

I retorted, "Look, I always listen to tapes and stuff for my ride in. You know that. They loaned me some, so I listened. It's no big deal. You've heard some of them also, and even thought they made sense to you."

She paused and smiled. "Hey, your vacation has started. I don't want it to begin with an argument about religion. I know whatever you decide about all of this will not be for a lack of effort or sincerity on your part. Mark, I have never seen anybody so dedicated to 'THE TRUTH.'" She held her hands up in quotation marks and said THE TRUTH sarcastically and then we both laughed. She continued, "Seriously, I just want you to find out what you need to know. God, I wish you could find peace about all of this. I do trust your ability to do research. I just don't want you to become brainwashed by all this Christian stuff. And you are becoming absorbed with it. You know how you can get so obsessive about things, and this is no exception."

"I know, Donna. I know. Don't worry. I'll get to the right place on this. I will."

"Okay, Mark, let's drop it for now."

The holidays went nicely. I enjoyed full days at the farm. I got enough wood together to last the rest of winter. We visited my brother and his family in town several times and enjoyed Christmas and New year's with them. The Bowl games are always a blast over there. All in all, the holidays provided good rest, family, and fun for a couple of weeks. I tried to take a vacation from my spiritual struggles.

A rather curious question did cross my mind, however. As I watched the sphere at Times Square falling into New Year's Day, something dawned on me. It was now 1987, but where did that number come from? Why had everybody centered history around somebody who lived some 2000 years ago? Oh, ye relentless search.

But what do I see on the horizon? Is this the answer that doth approach? Ah, sweet mystery of life, am I about to find you?

Chapter 7

Starry, Starry Night

When I went back to work, I also went back to apologetics' tapes and Christians. The problems started up again. More and more, I had a need to discuss this growing disturbance in my soul. Less and less, Donna wanted to hear about it, but she was sympathetic to the fact that I was having such a struggle. She just wasn't sympathetic to the cause of my trouble.

Tom, my Christian doctor friend was making almost daily visits to my lab, dropping gems of irrevocable logic into my mind and heart. One day we were discussing creation and organic origins. I had just isolated some protein compounds from rat livers to be used in some experiments later that month.

He asked, "Where are you going to keep those until you need them?"

I answered, "You know that. In the minus seventy freezer. Why? What are you getting at now?"

He responded, "Curious, isn't it? Organic origin evolutionists say protein-like compounds were generated in a primordial soup under intense heat; and, in those conditions complexity increased and stabilized into nucleic acids and on upwards into complex life forms. They say your great goo-golplex granddad was a paramecium, and his was carbon and ammonia. Yet you must now store these same types of compounds at minus seventy in order to maintain their viability for just a few weeks. It makes one wonder how they survived the primordial soup and all that heat, doesn't it?"

I was stopped dead in my tracks on that one. Even if evolution was plausible, the origins of organic life could not be explained within the framework of our known parameters. The good doctor had made his point. How could early deli-cate life chemicals survive the environment or-ganic origin theorists claim necessarily existed in order to bring about those chemicals? It requires DNA to replicate DNA. The first DNA had to come from somewhere! And I don't think Francis Crick's 'directed panspermia' is a very good explanation. Really now, an alien sperm from outer space that somehow infused into a pre-human species. And

Crick is a brilliant scientist! Lord, metaphysical and naturalistic explanations were getting embarrassing. This whole affair amounted to a Catch-22 against a simple materialistic origin to life. It took more faith to believe in the origins of life without an outside creator than to include one in the formula.

Tom added, "Have you ever considered the number of changes that must happen simultaneously in order for a species to evolve into a more complex and more advantageous creature? Why was sight necessary, for instance, and what were the odds of this 'mutation' taking place in history just when it was needed and in several species all at the same time? This question greatly plagued Darwin, you know."

I was dumbfounded. My God, this was so simple and obvious. I fought the anger as I realized I had been brainwashed as an undergrad in biology and biochem. I even made an 'A' in Evolution. How common it is that we humans take so long to overcome false assumptions because of pride, laziness, or phony precepts seen as more than precepts. Tom's simple proposal of statistical probability against advantageous spontaneous mutation made evolution itself seem like an adult fairy tale. In order to mutate into a higher life form, several advantageous variable changes would have to be made in a species at the same time environmental factors dictated its necessity. The odds against this happening in even one simple life form were astronomical! They were absolutely impossible odds when it came to all the complex life forms. Here was another lie I had embraced out of laziness and the prejudice of my personal philosophy. How foolish I felt.

But, wait a minute! This wasn't a problem. I wasn't an atheist. I was just a deist or a pantheist. I could accept a spiritual dimension to the origin of life. What was I getting so worked up about. Whew! That was close. I had no problem rejecting a chance materialistic organic origin to life in the universe. I knew there was a conscious order to creation. That is the reason I had left my agnosticism behind in the first place during my early undergraduate years. But then Tom added another quirky kink to my reality.

He said, "Now do not answer this right away, but please think about something. Is the nature of intelligent life personal or impersonal? If personal, which seems obvious, then what does that say about the original source of all life?"

I looked at him a bit puzzled.

Tom went on, "In other words, Mark, does the design which is clearly evident in the universe indicate accident or a designer behind the project.

Does the definition of designer encompass the personal or the impersonal? Just think about it. Okay?"

He was kind to say that, because I did not have an immediate answer. I knew what he was intimating. That since intelligent life is personal and since the origins of life could not be explained simply from a materialistic point of view, then isn't the source of creation also personal? It was irritating because it was a logical progression that amounted to a brick wall against my metaphysical path to any rational ends. How could I claim to have the divine spark within me and yet think of the divine oversoul as impersonal, seeing how I was very personal, along with every other human being? If I was like God, why was I an intelligence of personal interaction with other such beings, if this God of mine was an impersonal force? If my personal existence is just an illusion, then why does the very nature of illusion include the personal aspect? If I was to evolve into becoming nothing, how could I explain that I was already the essence of God since giving an explanation requires rational thought of an individual personality? This nonsense could go on and on, and that is where Tom knew I would go with it. I literally laughed at myself for thinking personal spiritual growth meant I was to become impersonal. Funny as it was, this mind game was most disturbing to my new age world view. Surely there was a gap in there somewhere. Surely. I just couldn't find it right then and there. As a matter of fact, I never did resolve this deductive observation with mysticism.

Then Tom made it even worse. He added, "One more thing. Do you know what the universal redshift is?"

I answered, "Yes. It's the Doppler effect on light. The exterior expanding portion of the universe shifts light down in frequency. Sort of like a horn when a car drives by. It's just with light instead of sound. So, from our vantage point, the light of those stars is shifted toward the red end of the visible spectrum. Why? What now?" I joked as though I was exasperated, though I usually was with Tom's pro-Christian logic.

Tom laughed at my guarded countenance and replied, "Man, I really enjoy giving witness to an enlightened and educated pagan. You're making this so easy and delightful."

I mocked up a groaning, grimacing smile at his glee, making the sound of a perturbed bull snorting out a deep, "Hmmph."

Tom continued, "Listen, it's just a thought, but if that universal matter on the outer regions is moving faster than our solar system, it seems logical that some of that mass will escape the gravitational pull from the rest of the universe. Right?"

I nodded my head in agreement with a look that said, "So?"

Tom continued, "If so, then eventually, all the matter will expand into nothingness, and the universe would grow cold. Absolute zero. Zilch."

I thought about it and mused, "Well, yes. A bit disturbing, but sounds logical. Why?"

His idiotic beeper went off just then, as he said, "Time travels infinitely into the future, but what about considering time backwards into an infinite past? Listen, I gotta go answer this call, but that's just another thing to think about. See ya later, Mark."

"Okay, Tom. See ya."

My wheels were already spinning on this one. I checked my TLC plates and saw I had about five minutes before they needed the radioactive scanner. So, I sat down with a piece of paper and drew a circle. I then drew it shattering as in the Big Bang. I did a series of sketches showing the matter from the original sphere collapsing back on itself for another cycle of Bang-expansion-recollapsing, leaving out a certain per cent of the original mass each time. Of course, this cyclical Big Bang of ultra-concentration and expansion is unlikely, but I wanted to give every opportunity to dispel where Tom knew I would go with this. Obviously, in theory, there would eventually be no centralized mass left, and the universe would grow cold, absolute zero, and die as infinitely frozen sub-atomic matter. Forever death - the result of limited energy and mass amidst unlimited space and time. Then I went backwards in time an infinite number of years, and got to the point I knew Tom wanted me to be. Our present moment would already be absolute zero if the physical universe as we know it had always existed, because an infinite number of years and Big Bang-expansion cycles would have already been reached, and the universe would be dead. The universe wasn't dead, so it had to have an origin, or at least an external source of energy not closed within our known universe. And that specific origin could not be explained by simple materialistic organic theories. Even using modern quantum physics to explain a constant generation of mass and energy into the universe amounted to philosophy and not science. There had to be a creation, an origin, and it had to have been directed.

This was great! Whatever my conclusions about Christianity, I knew there was more to the universe than meets the eye, just as I had subjectively concluded so often while meditating or listening to music. Only this time, the conclusion was more than subjective thought. Here was objective and deductive reasoning that would make Sherlock Holmes proud. I had a new peace that eternal death and nothingness would not be my destiny. This conceptual observation both comforted and intrigued me (so much so that eight years later, I used it as the basis for my graduate entry paper into Oxford University).

However, coupled with this was also something most challenging. It was Tom's question regarding the personal nature of intelligent life. Since the universe and life both had origins rationally demonstrated to be from outside of themselves, what was the nature of that source - personal or impersonal? Could a cosmic generator, or impersonal law, some mindless force, be the creator of the rationally constructed universe studied on a personal level by the intelligence we called Homo Sapiens? The answer seemed no, and this meant my pantheistic mysticism was looking pretty unfounded. The Force of Star Wars appeared to be an inadequate explanation as the source of personal, intelligent life in a universe of reliable rational laws of physics and thermodynamics.

The tension between my belief system and my research was becoming almost more than my mind could tolerate. It was about to divide Donna and me as well. She was most concerned about my mental health, but more irritated by my findings supporting the reasonableness of Christianity. For the first and only time in my life, I truly questioned whether or not I was going crazy. Donna was compassionate during this time but hated Christianity now more than ever because she saw it messing with my mind. Still, she respected my objective integrity and research abilities, so some of her distress was also brought on by the fact that she knew the Christian faith might not be such an illogical explanation for the ills of the world. Furthermore, she saw it as possibly a reasonable solution for man's destiny. That is the kind of intrusive thought that a mystic finds infuriating. She held firmly to mysticism. I just held to the image of peace and enlightenment in my meditations. I affirmed that my disturbances were some kind of spiritual storm before the permanent stillness that comes from the tranquillity of knowing all. Nirvana was near. Cosmic consciousness was coming. I had to believe that peace would soon be my constant companion. Such was my only hope at that time.

Since I usually drove into Vandy after lunch, I worked late into the evening most nights. At those quiet moments, I found myself reading bits and pieces of the Bible in order to find errors in its unity and philosophical presentation. These little sessions were not resulting in my rejecting it the way I thought that they would. It was as if some power was directing me to certain scriptures which shook the very foundations of my metaphysics. It was also as if this power was infinite, yet personal, not an impersonal Force. Of course, I refused to believe that, but I kept running across such verses nonetheless.

Comfort was not increased by the Bible's description of Satan as the god of Forces. This reminded me of 'the Force' of Star Wars, and my AMO instructions of becoming one with the 'Power of the Universe.' Somewhat distressing. The first chapter of second Peter assaulted my belief that I had been privy to the proper interpretation of the Bible through Unity Church and the AMO - "Know this first, that no prophecy of the scripture is of any private interpretation." The Bible's description of Satan deceptively appearing as an angel of light in the eleventh chapter of second Corinthians prompted me to consider that there really was such a rebellious angel with legions to deceive mankind with false doctrines. Doctrines such as mine? Doctrines referred to as Light and Magical Arts conveyed by spiritual beings of another dimension? Shakespeare said that a rose by any other name is still a rose. So is the destroyer. What if these as-

215

cended masters with whom I engaged were something else other than what they claimed. Such considerations made me shudder with the possibilities.

What or who had I really encountered that Christmas morning when I was seventeen? What was the real reason I always felt a sense of dread when I thought I was in the presence of ascended masters? In reality, what were those beings? The Bible never described an encounter with God as something confusing. It was often terrifying, but the recipient always knew it was God. Satan was described as the source of confusion. And I was definitely confused about my spirit encounters. The sixth chapter of Ephesians described my mind as a battleground between biblical truth and false teachings - "For we wrestle not against flesh and blood, but against principalities, against powers, against the rulers of the darkness of this world, against spiritual wickedness in high places."

Even if this evil was impersonal, without the biblical character known as Satan or the demons, rejected by most Methodists as I recalled from my childhood, there was still evil in this world. This was a concept I had denied with my mystical belief in unity, as opposed to the concept of duality of mind and body, of good and evil, of natural and supernatural. I had also been taught through my occult studies that we all had within us the Christ

216

consciousness, and that many teachers have lived throughout the centuries to teach us how to attain it. This grated against the twenty-fourth chapter of Matthew. "For many shall come in my name, saying I am Christ, and shall deceive many." For a brief moment, I humbled myself into considering that I was capable of being drastically deceived. Then my whole body shuddered and I pushed the Bible away. I stood up and began pacing around the lab. Yet, within a minute, I was back at my desk reading the Bible again.

Peter's second epistle made me think about the hundreds of witnesses who testified to the resurrection of Christ, many of whom had died for that testimony - "For we have not followed cunningly devised fables, when we made known unto you the power and coming of our Lord Jesus Christ, but were eyewitnesses of his majesty." These people had not died for what they knew to be a lie, but for what they believed to be the truth. It seemed unreasonable that they had all had a mass hallucination about the teachings, miracles, and resurrection. I recalled the old adage of one man saying he believed all prophets of history and the other replying that he believed in all prophets who had resurrected from the dead.

Why was Jesus crucified, if he was simply teaching the same basic thing that others were teaching? Christianity had such humble beginnings. It should have died off as had other movements with no royal support on earth. The socio-historical reasons alone could not suffice as an explanation for the spread of its message, and the benefits and abuse that have resulted from it through the centuries. How did it develop such a power base so quickly in terms of human history? I tossed and turned between nightmares wrestling with such questions.

The literary and textual studies into the historicity of the Bible and the related eyewitnesses were no help to my mysticism. I had learned that the extant records of extra-biblical material are the most numerous of any ancient writing. They also supported the biblical text to an astounding depth. I read a book by Simon Greenleaf, a nineteenth century attorney who was converted to Christianity on the weight of the evidence. It was profoundly convincing in its legal approach to the verification of the historicity of Jesus and his teachings and how they correlate with the common sense interpretation of the Bible.

I was definitely reaching a point of belief schizophrenia. I had encountered so much hope when mysticism first came into my life. I considered it to have been a good friend. Furthermore, I had forsaken many things and invested greatly in my efforts to gain the truth from metaphysics. I had also taught so many people these same beliefs, concepts, and principles by which I tried to live and evolve. Such seemed impossible to abandon, especially after so much effort and commitment. But logic was pointing another direction now. And at times, I felt a pull on my heart as well as my mind. The more I resisted that pull, the crazier I felt.

I still recall a birthday card for my 33rd birthday that Donna gave me. February 23, 1987. It read, "So you think you are losing your mind? Don't worry. I just want your body." We got a good laugh out of that, but the relevance was all too serious. I was in pretty bad shape mentally, struggling and battling for truth and sanity in a spiritual realm way out of my league. I would try to spend out my energy doing karate kicks and strikes on the punching bag, sometimes drenched in sweat and collapsing with exhaustion. I almost felt like a pawn in some great war, though I knew that must be a ridiculous analogy to a guy simply trying to figure a few things out.

A week later, I had just finished a discussion about constitutional law with Ginny and Liz. They suggested I read Romans, since I was so interested in law, informing me that Paul spoke a lot about that subject in that letter. That night, for the first time, I read a complete epistle from start to finish without stopping. As the end of the letter approached, I had a strange feeling of peace. "The grace of our Lord Jesus Christ be with you ..." From that point to the finish of the letter four verses later, I sensed a presence that was not like the one that always filled me with me fear. It was as if there was an entity waiting for an invitation, and giving one. I read the last verse, closed the Bible, and drew a deep breath. Calmly exhaling, I thought, "Wow! That was incredible. Why do I feel such peace?" I then rejected the presence, and tried to reject the words I had just read. But the emptiness that had accompanied me for so many years felt a little less empty. This was a new sensation, but I tried to ignore it as the result of a fatigued mind and heart. I finished up the evening's work, locked up the lab, and walked to my truck in a daze of thought.

The journey home that night topped them all. It was a non-stop flood of clear considerations. For some reason, I was perusing events throughout my post-modern journey. When I first started, it was a self-absorbed quest for power, not truth. When that became less of a thrill after so many psychic encounters, a need to understand overtook a need to experience. But what I had to admit was that it was self, not truth, that first led me into this quest. And then that truth was in the realm of absolute or relative was an issue. But I took that to its rational (irrational?) conclusion, and realized that all questions were ultimately meaningless if all was indeed relative. To ignore common sense on that issue was embarrassing. Of course there are absolutes. Any scientist knows that. To say otherwise in the name of tolerance is not intellectual, it is cowardly, lazy, and void of integrity.

That entity I had encountered at Christmas when I was seventeen was not the least bit comforting, and I had to further admit that my feeling of dread never did ease in the presence of the power I thought I wanted. Why? If it was so right, why was I so repulsed with an instinctive aversion? If my instincts were wrong, how could I call myself attuned and basically divine?

For the sake of argument, I considered the possibility that my astral experiences might have come from an evil source. Verification of their reality was not enough to determine they were divinely inspired or basically good in nature. The Bible did say Satan could appear as an angel of light and that he was the prince and power of the air. Then there was the time I saw the message on the blackboard. I could have seen those messages before my nap that day; but, what is worse is that they could have been communicated to me from a dark spiritual realm to deceive me into thinking I was developing a great power. That was not a very comforting thought. I felt like I had been sleeping in a one-room cabin in the wilderness, only to discover a huge nest of rattlesnakes right next to my bed. My hands tightened on the steering wheel and I gave a shiver. I tried to shrug off this feeling as a chill ran down my spine.

I remembered Chin and that memorable afternoon of blind-blocking karate. Surely, he hadn't tricked me and thrown his punches where my blocks were placed. Surely it wasn't just a fluke. Perhaps that too could be explained from a region of the spirit world whose sole purpose was to steer me away from something more important. Perhaps that is why it frightened me so. Then again, perhaps it was nothing significant at all. Oh, I was just so weary from thinking about all of this! The image of the ascended master who had warned me of this battle came to mind. Was he warning me out of love, or was he trying to prevent me from knowing the truth. I shuddered again and again with the possibilities of my many encounters.

What was clear was that it was a very real possibility that all of those experiences could have very well come from the enemy of God as described by the Bible. Was "Disobey, live forever and ye shall be as gods" the first great lie? Was "There are no absolutes which require obedience" another phrasing of this same basic position? Perhaps the devil's greatest deception was that he didn't exist. A cartoon character can do no harm. A myth is not out to lead us astray. A fantasy of some ancient religious fanatic could not live in today's world. But such camouflage could make the danger blend into its surroundings. The enemy that travels at night approaches under the cover of darkness. The mugger hides in the shadows. The poison is sweetened with honey. A half-truth is less obvious than a lie. A counterfeit heaven half-way along the journey to the real thing could be mistaken as the goal. What would be even worse is if this counterfeit was the half-way point on a journey to hell! I resisted this whole idea. I couldn't be that stupid. I couldn't be that easily deceived. My pride told me, "Impossible!" I verbalized a couple of curse words followed by a boastful and defiant, "No way!"

But I had to admit that I had been challenged, even excited that Christianity did not require a mindless faith. Christianity was not striving to be beyond the senses or beyond reason, as in mysticism, metaphysics, and the occult. This reminded me of the third chapter of Peter's first letter. "Always be ready to make a defense to anybody who asks so you can give a reason for your hope, yet with gentleness and reverence." In fact, I had learned that much of the modern scientific method had Christian roots. According to Christianity, a personal rational God created a rational universe that could be studied by personal intelligence to understand reliable results, consistent laws, and verifiable corroboration. I had also become impressed with the simplicity of the gospel message. That night, I recognized that the basic gospel message and Christianity's claim of exclusivity were not demonstrations of intolerance, but were essential elements of a religion that seemed to explain very well most of the world's ills.

I was forced to ask the question as posed so eloquently by C. S. Lewis, "Is Jesus God, a lunatic, or a liar?" After all, this Christ was a Jew, and he did claim to forgive sins, and to a Jew, only God could forgive sins. And the Jews did not believe in any kind of multi-theistic mysticism. Trying to rewrite religious and scriptural history around a mystical worldview was dishonest and poor scholarship. There was no way around it. There was no way to pretend anything less of the stark position of that carpenter around whom we had centered time. This Jesus had claimed to be the one and only God, and history had not proven him to be a liar or a lunatic.

The considerations continued as my little

truck whirred down the interstate. It did seem that re-incarnation provided a more fair means of opportunity in light of the variety of unjust circumstances upon the planet. But the Christians were the first to admit that injustice was to be found everywhere. That was their point. The earth was no longer paradise, and the evil of injustice was another example along with the love of money and other deadly sins. Things were not fair because this was not the Garden of Eden. This is why a corrective measure was needed. The universe was in the process of reconciliation back to the Creator by the work of the cross. This work would reach its final consummation at the second coming of Christ. When I would ask them how it could be fair that some poor kid in Africa starves to death before he could speak, they would respond that it wasn't fair. I hated that, because it was so simplistic, yet it also meant there were things beyond my own personal level of wisdom. Were they rationalizing or was I being too proud, arrogantly assuming that I could decide the best explanation for the atrocities and inequalities that plague our planet?

I was forced to admit the cruelty of a doctrine that says success in life comes from right thinking and failure and sickness come from wrong or sinful thinking. The guilt and embarrassment that would bring upon people in need was almost unbearable. To be sure, I knew there was much an individual could do to improve his life, and I believed in personal initiative and responsibility. But Christianity seemed more compassionate and reasonable to those who were truly doing their best and still suffering all kinds of evil and misfortune. The countries dominated by Hinduism had some of the worst poverty levels in the world, largely due to a belief in personal karma. Was this truly an illusion, or was the poor kid with the bloated belly really starving and slowly deteriorating in a miserable death? It would be nice to shuffle it off as karma, but not very kind. How loving, evolved, and progressive could that be? There was a reason the Christian based western world had delivered more charity than all of history combined.

That night, I saw the concept of eternal life through grace as an affront only to my pride and not as an affront to reason. The occult had taught me to ignore the desires of my heart regarding a desire for the truth. But the Bible had promised that God would grant such desires of the heart. The God of the Bible seemed an easy choice on that one. All in all, I knew I wanted the truth, not Bible-believing Christianity; but, all my efforts were leading to the conclusion that they were one and the same.

Over the next few days, the battle within my

mind and heart became so intense that I actually thought suicide might be nice just to give me some rest. Of course, I was not really considering it, but something had to be done. Something! Anything! My heart cried out, "If anybody or anything is out there, somewhere, please help me. Please."

Then came my forever special night in Nashville. It was typically cool and crisp for March. Donna and Ted and I were walking around Vanderbilt's campus. I was sharing the desperation of my circumstances. I pleaded with them to help me resolve this, but they could not. No advice, no comfort, no amount of concern, genuine or not, could help. I felt as though I could not go on, yet I knew that I must. I felt I might soon start hallucinating or going blind or drooling or something because I thought I would be ready for an institution any second now. I was shivering from the chill in the air and the fear in my soul. We decided to get out of the night air for a while. So we entered the open basement door of a building to warm up a bit.

As I stepped through the door into the warmth, there was a Presence that ignited a flame deep within my soul. This Presence was awesome, yet not fearful. He was compelling, yet not demanding. I was motionless, though not with fear. I was quiescent with peace. Speaking to me out of love,

He said "You know. I am the Truth." I heard that clearly in my mind and heart.

My wrestling ceased with the joy of absolute assurance. I felt no chaos or confusion. There were no questions about the message or the messenger. In fact the messenger was the message. Truth. I knew this presence was not an it, but a personal being. His name was Jesus. Years of empty, aching, yearning, searching, pain flowed out of my heart to be filled by the Holy Spirit of the one and only Source of all goodness. Unashamedly, right in front of my two skeptical companions, I did the only thing I had to do to embrace fully what I already knew to be the truth.

I quietly accepted Jesus into my heart. I simply whispered, "Thank-you." With that simple expression, out flowed the tension. Donna and Ted thought I had gone over the edge of insanity. The truth is that I was now more sane than ever before. They had witnessed the changing expressions in my soul that showed on my face. From desperate struggle to perplexed bewilderment to contemplation to a final token resistance to acceptance, understanding, joy, and peace. I looked at each of them, and revealed such a smile as they had never seen on my face. Rather anti-climactic in some ways, yet totally appropriate considering the focus shifted from Self to Self's Creator. It's not the ego-stroking glory material of Hollywood movies, but it's the stuff of love at the essence and core of the universe, the true reality of all being. Enlightenment. Christ consciousness was revealed as becoming conscious of Christ, and the truth regarding the Truth.

As my eyes welled up, revealing the pure emotion of absolute joy, I let my pride and unfounded commitment to lies and deceit flow out of my heart. They were replaced by the presence of the Holy Spirit. I had not found the truth. The Truth had found me, for the Truth was not a concept or a principle or a force. The Truth was He who had described himself as the way, the truth, and the life. The Truth was a real, personal Being who would forever be my Lord, Savior, and Friend. The Truth was Jesus Christ, the only true ascended Master of the Universe.

At that moment, the Lord Messiah did not slither into my life as had that ominous presence posing as an angel of light sixteen years earlier. My Savior came without disguise and has never left. I no longer had to seek the truth. He sought me out, and now I could daily and gladly seek His face. The goal for which I desperately hungered had been granted as a gift. My soul would never starve again. The bliss of enlightenment had become a reality. I now knew the Truth, and the

Truth had set me free. And the once empty place in my heart has been filled to overflowing.

Donna and I had a rather quiet drive home to the farm that night. No doubt she was wondering how long a mystic and a born-again Christian would last as a married couple. There were many ramifications from my new commitment flowing through her mind. I had a blissful fortress against such invasions. I was on a honeymoon and the door to the honeymoon suite was iron-clad. It is not that I was ignoring the real world. In fact, I saw reality clearly for the first time in my life. When we arrived at the farm, Donna expressed her exhaustion over the evening's events. Every cell in my body was wide awake. She told me she was genuinely happy for me, but I sensed her irritation. This evening disturbed her, but she was too tired to get into a heavy discussion. She went on to sleep as I continued to embrace the evening of my soul's birth.

It was hard to imagine that I had truly discovered the Truth, and what it turned out to be was such a surprise. But there was no denying it. It is so obvious to anyone once it is accepted. I was powerless and humble as I yielded in gratitude to the mercy. Precious freedom granted. Sweet mystery unveiled.

I had contained my emotions in front of Ted

and Donna. It was later that night, alone on the deck at the farm, that I fully released the tension built up from the seemingly endless quest that had finally come to a successful end. Once again, my gaze fell upon the magnificent spread of stars in the night sky, the same stars from decades earlier. I thought of that first carol I had learned as a toddler. I fell to my knees in thanks and worship as I raised my arms to the Giver of light, life, and love. For every effort, for every struggle, for each wayward path I had followed, there was now a tear of joy that streamed down my cheek, striking the deck upon which I knelt, and reflecting the starlight above for all the angels to see.

Chapter 8

The Last Enemy

A tranquil peace came with my achieved goal; but, there were more fireworks to come. I had a new enemy. He considered me a defector now. A traitor. After all, I had dined with him. I had worked among his ranks in his military outposts. I had trained alongside his legions and officers. I knew his weapons, his tactics, his plans, his disguises, and his lying doctrines. He was the god of Forces and he had no intention of allowing me to just walk away in peace without a forceful conflict.

His first target was Donna. She was still held in captivity behind enemy lines. She had been relieved for me the night of my deliverance; but, she thought this meant the end of our relationship. She had never seen such peace in my countenance, but she knew how the rule was laid out. Serious Christians and serious mystics could not be happily married. She thought we were no exceptions to this rule. Nonetheless, she did decide to hang around long enough to see if my peace and new truth would last. And sure enough, this was the real thing. She was a sensitive woman. She knew that my overflowing joy had a very real and true Source. But she thought I was confused about the nature of the Source.

The next three weeks saw dazzling bursts of spiritual energy at our farmhouse. Donna and I were at great odds over my conversion. One could almost hear the clash of supernatural swords. I knew the enemy all too well. Donna did not believe he existed. I knew the nature of Jesus Christ. Donna thought he was just another great avatar. I knew I had formerly been separated from God, especially now that I experienced His presence. Donna's metaphysics were still what mine had been. No evil. No sin. No personal God from whom our sin separates us. The discussions and disagreements went on and on. As I look back on those three weeks, I realize the only reason I survived was because I was floating on the cloud of my new conversion to Christianity. I simply could not be rattled. I was truly enjoying the first love which Jesus speaks about in the Book of Revelation. Donna kept commenting on how calm and peaceful I was about it all. Most unusual.

Though I displayed the peace of God, inside I was also desperate for Donna to see the light. I began to stay up late into the night, kneeling by the bed in prayer. Donna would wake up and roll her eyes at me. She had to admit she was touched by my dedication and concern, but she really thought I was losing sleep to a hopeless cause. After several nights of such exchanges, she once woke up to the crackle of a spring storm's lightning outside. There I was, kneeling and praying. She had nothing humorous or sarcastic to say.

Her countenance was different this time. I could tell something had a profound effect upon this woman before me. It was a dream. Dream interpretation is a common practice in the post-modern spirituality. To this day, I can only assume God was meeting Donna where she was, just as he had done for me. Perhaps it was much in the same way that Jesus went to dine in the homes of unbelievers and sinners. He met them on their turf as he invaded the enemy's territory to claim it for the Father in Heaven.

In this particular dream, Donna said that there were many people waiting in a room for some great human dignity to arrive. She and I were among those in waiting. She was surprised to see Jesus enter the room, and he came and sat upon my lap. As he began to get up, I reached up and pulled him back down. Donna described the image to me with, "You just would not let go of him. I guess this means that even if it cost you everything, you would never give up your belief in Jesus." She paused, and added, "Even if I leave you."

This possibility made me very sad, but I answered her quite simply and directly with, "Yes, that's right. Never."

The next two nights had dreams of the same magnitude. The first was in the same room again. Only this time, Jesus came to Donna. He knelt down where she was seated until his face was level with hers. He cupped her face in his hands, smiled as if he knew everything about her. She described to me how she felt in her dream at that point.

"Mark, I felt so ashamed at first. I began to cry with horrified self-loathing, but Jesus' eyes watered up with compassion. I knew he loved me. I had never felt such hope and acceptance." She sighed and smirked, "Leave it to me to meet the most remarkable man in my life in a dream."

"Very funny," I said as we both laughed. But then I looked at her rather seriously, wanting to speak some profound gem of wisdom. I honestly did not know what to say. Perhaps the Holy Spirit was clamping my big mouth shut. Quite an accomplishment considering how anxious I was to persuade

Donna with my own words. I remained silent.

Then Donna spoke softly, "Listen, I really don't want to talk about this anymore, okay? It's kinda freaking me out." She then chuckled with, " Man, what have you gotten into?"

I replied, "There is no mystical power from my prayers. I am just sharing my burden for you with the Master of the Universe. That's all. All that is happening is that God is reaching out to you. That's what this is all about. This is great stuff. Why don't you want to talk about it anymore?"

She answered, "I just don't. Okay? Look, I have felt sort of stressed out since your big conversion. I really don't know what to think about it just now. I really want to go back to sleep. I just thought I would tell you about the dream, that's all. But I don't want the discussion to go any further than it already has. Do you understand? Can you just accept that, please?"

I was in such a trusting state. I was on a honeymoon with the love of Christ. I had no problem just keeping my mouth shut at that time and letting God do his work on Donna. And keeping my mouth shut when I cared so deeply about something was a miracle in and of itself. Believe you me.

The third dream rather put a scare into Donna. She dreamed that she was with her younger sister.

They were shopping in Green Hills in Nashville. There was a flood running down Hillsboro Road and covering the entire city. Something inside of her told her there were worldwide catastrophes, and that the end of the world was near. But the waters receded, and her sister told her everything was fine as she joined a colorful parade of happy-go-lucky passers by. Donna knew in her dream that it was not okay, and desperately tried to convince her sister to get out of the parade. She tried to make her understand that Christ was the only way to be saved from the final destruction. After Donna woke up, she was amazed that she had taken such a position, even in her wildest dreams.

She said, "Mark, I think I would like to request that you stop these prayers by our bed every night. I can't take any more of this stuff."

"It is not my prayers, Donna. It's God. He's calling you."

She paused. I noticed a hint of tears in her eyes. Then I was amazed at what she said next.

She said, "I know."

I was stunned. At first I stared in disbelief, but then I asked a doubtful, "What?"

"You heard me." She gave out a big long-winded sigh. "I know he is calling me. I just don't know if I can believe like you do. I am a truth student."

I felt so sorry for her, because I knew exactly

how she must be torn. Christianity means spiritual death to a serious mystical truth student. But she turned out to be much wiser than me. She could always cut to the essentials. I fought the call of God's truth for a very long time. It was different with Donna. Though she resisted at first, it was only a few more days after her third dream before she was also being baptized into the truth. Literally. I was overflowing with happiness as she came up out of the baptismal waters. Ginny and Liz were there to witness this expression of the miracle of faith. From that moment, a new and soft peace was imbued into Donna's character. A few nights earlier, Donna had experienced the one pure thing she wanted to see before she died. She had accepted him into her heart as Stan and I were reading from Philippians and Revelation at his apartment. Now, she was experiencing the same joy felt by the first members of God's church as they were baptized!

A final direct assault by fear from the enemy occurred that very night. We drove back to the farm late, ecstatic over our new-found faith. We were quite joyous and exhausted as we entered slumber. At three in the morning, while I was sleeping, I felt a familiar, uncomfortable presence. I can easily remember how it was invading my euphoria. This couldn't be! The familiar dread that accompanied so many of my mystic visitations. It was terrifying. I sat straight up in bed as I awoke with a start. Donna had also waked up and heard in her mind, "Something evil this way comes." She could hear the sinister phrase repeating itself. But my fear turned to righteous indignation. I suddenly remembered what I was now and who my Savior was. I began to pray out loud and calling on Him. Donna and I both heard a loud sound that seemed to smack twenty feet from our bed. We looked at each other and smiled. Peace. Peace. Silent night. Holy night. Christ had not tolerated the invasion. Every fiber of my being was filled with peace. I know other believers who have come out of a similar religious search as mine who occasionally wrestle with fear. With some, it can go on for a long time, and be very intense. I feel blessed that I have never had another such experience. Donna and I felt so protected by our Lord that night.

A few months after the Holy Spirit had conceived in our hearts, a baby was conceived in Donna's womb. I had a vasectomy reversal shortly before then. We had a 40 per cent chance of conceiving after a year. The doctors were pleasantly surprised to see a pregnancy only a couple of months after the procedure. The night before our son was born, we still had not decided upon a name.

As we were reading from our favorite prophet, Isaiah, the name became rather obvious. Duh? Sometimes I think I know why God calls us his sheep. Isaiah was born by C-section the next morning, because complications began to develop. But all was well. With the pregnancy, that is.

A financial crisis had come upon us a week before Isaiah was born. It was a disagreement with the taxman. A stranglehold was put on my cash flow. This caused me to wrestle early in my Christian walk with questions about God's provision. We would have lost our farm, had it not been for the loving intervention of a fellow saint. Faith was aided by the love of a few elders, particularly one who gave me some extra work so I could feed my family. It was a difficult time, but recovery finally came. However, that was not the end of our trouble.

That financial situation was working itself out rather nicely. All things seemed to be falling into place. We had found a good country church where we could worship. And it was only minutes from our farm. On the day we were celebrating Isaiah's first birthday, we were also excited that in a few more months, we would be having another baby. But that night brought us some concerns. After Isaiah had gone to sleep, Donna revealed to me what she had discovered. In hindsight now, it seems almost absurd that the next year and a half of difficulty began with such a little thing. And that it was also the beginning of years of torment to follow. A lump. A simple little mass under the skin.

"It's just a lump," I said. "These things are almost always benign."

However, in the next couple of weeks, Donna was diagnosed with breast cancer five months into the pregnancy of our second child. A radical mastectomy was performed several weeks later. One month after the surgery, we lost little Samuel while he was still in the womb. The first round of chemotherapy immediately ensued, since we had been postponing it until Samuel was born. The chemotherapy made Donna quite ill. However, we thought all was well, because there were no further signs of the cancer, and the thirty-three lymph nodes checked from the surgery were all clean. We were left to grieve the loss of Samuel, and to deal with the grief that accompanies a radical mastectomy.

In spite of the difficulties, we had a Christmas of celebration. The financial crisis was behind us. Isaiah was healthy and growing. Donna's cancer seemed to have been stopped before it could spread in her body to fatal proportions. No doubt things could have certainly been easier since we became Christians, but we were thankful to know the truth and to have the blessings of health and life. The celebration lasted two weeks.

Shortly after New Year's Day, Donna decided to get an X-ray for a sore rib. She injured it during the holidays when she slipped on some ice at the farm. There was a deep pain that would not let up. Upon receiving the results of the X-rays, the ribs looked fine. The thirteen spots on the lungs looked very bad. The cancer had indeed spread to them. I was stunned with the oncologist's phone call that afternoon.

He said, "Mark, you need to know what this means. It may be a year or two, possibly more, or as soon as a few months. But sooner or later, this cancer will get her. I suspect within the year she will die. You best get things in order for this."

I paused, breathless on the other end of the phone line.

He added, "Am I going too fast for you?"

I replied, "Yes, maybe you are. I, uh, I uh. I want to say I don't understand, but, hum, I think I do." I blew out a long breath and added, "Wow."

"I am sorry, Mark. I did not mean to shock you so badly."

"Is there any way to deliver such a summation without a shock?"

"No, I guess not. Do you want to discuss further treatments now?"

"No, no, thanks. I will call you about that tomorrow. I couldn't possibly do anything else beyond surviving the drive home tonight. How much does Donna know?"

"Only that it has spread to the lungs. I haven't been so clear with her about the impending consequences. I thought that best be left to you if that is what you want. Otherwise, I will be glad to call her back and discuss the situation."

"No, that's okay. You did the right thing. I will handle that. Thanks. I'll call you tomorrow."

"Okay, Mark. I am so very sorry."

"Yes, thanks. We'll talk tomorrow. Bye."

"Good-bye, Mark."

I placed the phone back on the receiver and looked over at my experiment running on my bench. I walked over to the window and looked out from my eighth floor lab. My eyes perused the rest of Vanderbilt's vast research complex. Then I thought of all such institutions all over America, and then all over the world. I shook my head thinking of how many were working on prevention and cure of breast cancer, and how long this had been going on. But then my mind went beyond the efforts of mankind, and I spoke out loud to my Creator.

"God, what is this all about? I don't mean to sound faithless or ungrateful, but this seems pretty crummy. I feel really bad right now. I am confused. Lord, what are you doing here with this situation?"

This was all going too fast for me. When I saw Donna that night, she was in shock and denial as I was. She had only gone into the doctor's that day to X-ray her ribs. We were not expecting this. We had rented a movie a day earlier. What dark prophecy it seemed that turned out to be. She cried as we watched Bambi with Isaiah that night. It became obvious that I would not have to tell her the doctors' view of the consequences of this new medical information.

She turned to me, and fighting her denial, she spoke through her tears. "Isaiah is going to be Bambi. But Samuel in heaven won't be anymore." We chuckled, because that was a light and silly kind of thing to say. However, the morbid nature of what she meant was all to heavy and serious.

"It will be okay. We can beat this thing," I said as I lied to us both. But was this really a lie. Maybe we couldn't beat it, but God certainly could. We then prayed.

After Donna went to sleep, I wept. I cried to my Savior, "God, this just can't be! Please! Wake us up from this nightmare. Please help. Please help. Please, Lord."

Donna was courageous over the next few months as more intense chemo began. One day, she called me from the grocery store. The desperation in her voice was chilling. I knew something was seriously wrong. She had barely managed to get to a phone and dial home. She was dizzy and could not see well. Her head was splitting and she had tunnel vision. I picked her up and took her to the hospital. The brain scans revealed that the cancer had spread to the brain. That was in May. After more chemotherapy and radiation, things did not improve. By October, she had become bed-ridden.

One day, I sat by her bedside, holding her hand. A deep fear stirred within me. As I stared at her with confidence and reassurance, inside I was most disturbed and insecure. What was that terrible thing I felt? I could sense the life slipping away from her. Had she given up? Or had she just been through the classic stages of dying? Shock, denial, anger, depression, and now ... acceptance. She was so sad about leaving Isaiah behind at his tender age. This idea tormented her so. Yet she had peace about her immortality. I wondered if she was developing peace about all of this?

I stared at her face that day. Their was a peculiar blue tint to her green eyes. Maybe it was a result of all the treatments, maybe the lighting, maybe just the tears in my own. I stared at her face that day. I wanted to memorize it. This was not the slender beauty I had married. The chemo had ripped out all of her hair. The radiation had burned her skin. The prednisone had puffed out her face. No, this was not the physical beauty I had married, but this was a woman whose face I wanted to memorize. A face of courage and dignity amidst the fire of the humiliation of a debilitating death of agony. That is the inspiration I wanted to remember forever, especially if she was to die soon.

If she was to die? But I had no room for such considerations. I just thought that my job as head of household was to keep the faith that God would deliver us from this. Oh, how I wanted God to lift this burden! But her labored breaths sounded a bit less full of life with each passing day.

However, I absolutely refused to believe she would die. Over the next few weeks, I continued to fast and pray. Elders came and anointed her with oil. 24-hour prayer chains were established. My faith was focused on a miracle recovery. I couldn't believe that she would die. I would not allow my faith to waiver even the least little bit. My God, my Lord, my Savior will intervene. He will put a stop to this terrible thing. Donna can't die. She just cannot die. God will heal her. She won't die. She can't. She won't!

"The last enemy to be abolished is death."

Donna Jean Boardman Phillips died on the morning of October 23, 1990. At that moment, she came face-to-face with the one pure thing she met and embraced several years earlier. Once, with spring in the air, she had accepted Jesus Christ into her mind and heart. Now, with autumn's colors abounding, He accepted her into His presence. The tree leaves were bursting forth with blood reds. How marvelous it is that they serve each year as a final reminder of what will follow winter. It colors the hope of life's resurrection that follows the cold, gray, lifeless time.

Isaiah was two and a half years old. We began the difficult process of recovery. We wrestled with grief, sadness, and anger. Though I knew the truth, I even struggled with keeping the faith. But the Truth remained faithful to me and kept me. Yet I felt hopeless. Had I lost that first love which I embraced during Donna's saving conversion through the cross of Christ? Could I no longer find comfort in words from Paul's epistle to the Romans? Wasn't this the same letter of the Bible that had moved me so deeply as I read through it in the lab only a few years earlier? "And hope does not disappoint us, because God has poured out his love into our hearts by the Holy Spirit, whom he has given us." I hoped Donna's cancer would go away. It did not. I prayed that God

248

would intervene and that Donna would be miraculously healed. She was not. I believed that the anointing oil of the elders of the church would somehow prevent her death. But she died. I fasted and prayed, trusted and believed. My hope was disappointed.

I was left hoping for survival through the relentless pain of bereavement. The sleepless nights. The never-ending days of sorrow. The images of her suffering. There were countless sights, sounds, and smells that would trigger memories and strange new feelings. They would hurt so deeply that I would double over in pain. An ambulance, a street, the weather, a commercial, a song. My sleeping son's face. The list could fill a book.

My hope became a cry for recovery. Sometimes it was a scream of anger. I wanted to practice karate on the next person who quoted me Romans 8:28! Sometimes my cry was a humiliated whimper, begging for merciful relief. Ultimately, it boiled down to one thing. I hoped for comfort from God. And ultimately, that hope was not disappointed. When I bitterly cried in desperation, God would hand me his handkerchief to dry my face and eyes. It was already damp and salty. "Jesus wept." It is the shortest and perhaps the most profound verse in the Bible when a person is doubled over in pain. "Jesus wept." The cloth was wet with the tears of God. He cries with us when we hurt. Is he still enraged at what He has defeated - death? Perhaps so, but only because we are still so devastated by its ravages, even though we have eternal hope and life.

Through my son's depression and my anger, could I continue to hope as a Christian? The whole family was grieving. I had no Christian friends well-versed in death, dying, and espousal bereavement. Most of my family members were back in Texas. Fortunately, my brother and his wife lived in Nashville with their two sons. They were of enormous comfort during this time. Isaiah and I spent every weekend at their house for a long time.

The first year was terrible. Every holiday and anniversary was the first in this new darkness of bereavement. The second year was made worse by the fact that so many people thought I should be 'well' by then. I even had an elder friend write to me that King David only officially grieved for a year in the Old Testament. An elder's wife left a stinging message on my phone recorder. She said I needed to snap out of it and get rid of my anger, that I was not the only one feeling pain in the world. Though such advice was meant to help, the ignorance of well-meaning people was often so painful and detrimental to my recovery. Such premature and ill-informed exhortation only increased my temptations toward faithless bitterness.

So how was I able to hang on, even if by a thin thread sometimes? Why did I return time and time again to hope as a Christian? It is the same reason I still do it. Mainly because Jesus resurrected on the third day after he went to the cross for you and me of His own free will. That is some serious, victorious love and mercy. I hope mainly for eternal glory bought by the precious blood of my Savior. But I also hope in this present time because He knows what being human is like. This results not only from divine wisdom, but from personal experience. He came to earth as the Word made flesh (John 1:1-18). He wept. He weeps with us now. He comforts us now. There are difficult struggles on this fallen earth at present. But all who have come to accept the Truth can look forward to an eternity with God and with one another, when there will be no more tears. The twenty-first chapter of Revelations is healing balm.

"He will wipe every tear from their eyes. There will be no more death or mourning or crying or pain, for the old order of things has passed away."

Epilogue to the Fellow Pilgrims

I have reaped many things, good and bad, from my journey, my quest for truth. But the end of my pursuit is what is important now. My mystical journey's end was the beginning of eternal life. No doubt the trek was often a battlefield and I suffered many war injuries along the way. But the fifty-third chapter of Isaiah promises that by the stripes of my Lord, our wounds are healed. Such is His mercy. Scars? Perhaps, as with all people. Yet they are reminders of the black battles from which I was delivered. Such marks serve to highlight the joy I have been given, a joy that is everlasting. No doubt there may be more as is the case for fellow travelers; but, the only scars I will know in eternity are those of the once tortured flesh of my Lord and Savior, who delivered his body to be broken for me. Such is His grace.

There are so many things that Christians can admire about metaphysical truth students, and even learn from them. Depth of sincerity and discipline. A willingness to exercise personal initiative. A desire to exchange ideas. This is speaking of the rank and file members of the loose-knit federation of post-modern spiritual seekers, and not necessarily of the leaders, many of whom became established in the earlier movements of the so-called New Age, now the new post-modern spirituality. In a new age truth student, one may often find an open mind receptive to ideas different from his own. There is usually a willingness to dialogue. The best way is to ask questions. Let them make the discoveries necessary to their eternal life. You can help point them in the right direction, but they are already searching by the fact that they are metaphysical truth students. One can be honest, objective, and sincere with such a disciple. They will be aware of your love and depth of commitment.

They carry prejudices, to be sure, but pilgrims on the path to enlightenment are generally approachable, because they are seeking and listening and trying to do that which is right. The problem is that their focus is most often wrong. It is self-improvement, self-growth, self-evolution to godhood. As pompous as that may sound, it also involves a deceptive sense of nobility. The nobility of responsibility. Yet it is a perverted understanding, because it denies that only God is truly noble.

We must remember that in the human mind and heart, Self is a powerful adversary to the rightful Heir of Heaven's throne. If divinity can be mine through enlightenment, why would I need a Savior?

But I remember a thought I had one day, shortly before accepting the Truth. It was that if someone died and left me a billion dollars, I would be a fool to reject it because I had not earned it myself (dangers of money-love aside). Likewise, I decided I would also be a fool to reject the eternal riches of glory if someone had died and resurrected for that inheritance. And billions of dollars are nothing compared to those blessings of forever.

It is a difficult blow to one's ego to admit that there are just certain things that one cannot accomplish by his own power and merit. It is humiliating to admit to being a beggar at heaven's temple gates. Pride does indeed go before the fall. Fortunately, my pride went and I fell ... to my knees. Thank God I am not heading for an eternity of darkness and separation from my loving Creator. I am an alien upon this planet now. I have taken up citizenship in another world.

It was in the spring that God had given me new life through His only begotten Son. It was seven years later that another rebirth came in springtime. It was a rebirth after almost dying of grief. On this new spring occasion, the Wonderful Counselor, the bright Morning Star guided Isaiah and me into the path of dear sweet Angela and her two wonderful children.

Isaiah and I were visiting the church my brother and his family attended. It was Palm Sunday. The children's choir was giving a special presentation. When my eyes fell on Angie, my heart skipped a beat, and I was breathless. As the sweet voices of the children assaulted the bitterness of grief that gripped my heart, God placed a love for the woman directing their harmony deep within my soul. This woman was my angel, Angela. A few months later, I married my true love. Our union created God's new blended family of five. Isabella, Isaiah, Isom, Angie, and Mark now share a life under His guidance. As I write this, we are currently residing in England, where I am completing graduate work in theological studies at Oxford University. The miracle of our union is unfolding. It is love and it is joy and it is all to His honor and glory. All of it. The laughter and the tears, the play and the work, the joy and the pain. Wow! Forgive me for name-dropping, but Angie and I are personal friends with the Creator of the universe. Our three children are also getting to know him pretty well. In fact, God often reveals some profound things through those little charges.

"Except ye be as little children ..."

There are no immunities from difficulties on this planet. Things can get so dark so quickly, and so often. History has proven that to be the nature of this world, just as the Bible describes it. However, there can be a personal peace that surpasses all understanding, though it is grounded in a reasonable belief. I sincerely and diligently searched for it, and now I am found. This tranquil peace is rooted in only one place. There are no other paths to enlightenment. There are no alternate routes to the realm of heaven. There is only one way, my friend. I should know. I feel as if I tried them all. Seek, ye pilgrim, seek. Ask, ye empty-heart, ask. Knock, ye weary searcher, knock upon the Door of Truth. Never give up until you know. Then, don't be afraid to fall on your knees. Call His name out loud ... then stop ... then listen. You are invited. Join the fellowship in the eternal feast. Come on in for a swim in the river of life. The water of Truth is clear, defined, precious, and fine. Then bask on the shores of eternal life. The sunshine of heaven is the best ever to warm your soul.

GLOSSARY

S ome of the terms and concepts encountered throughout this book might need some clari fication to make your reading more mean-ingful and enjoyable. Thus, I have provided this short glossary which I hope will be helpful as you peruse your way through this journey.

Age of Aquarius (Aquarian thought) - This is a broad term describing the New Age vision that a time of world-wide peace and universal enlighten-ment is now being ushered into planet earth. This term also represents a deeply held religious con-viction for many individuals. The planetary vi-sion and one's personal spiritual evolution are un-deniably connected. The age preceding this one was Pisces. This is why the fish was the symbol of Christianity. The general consensus of most New Age adherents is that we are currently liv-ing on the border-line of time between these two ages, awaiting a close and imminent transforma-tion into the new age.

Arcane - In reference to mysticism, this is that knowledge which is imparted to only a few. It can be secret knowledge or private interpretation of holy writings which are public. This second idea was behind my Bible-teaching sessions on re-incarnation at Unity church. The instructions I received through the Order were also considered arcane. If we take this word back to Latin *arcanus* (hidden) and *arca* (chest), what comes to mind is the arc of the covenant in the Old Testament. Many mystics understand that this arc was full of secret knowledge and power. This brings to mind that dramatic scene of special effects in the first 'Indiana Jones' motion picture, when the arc was opened to the destruction of those present. Arcane knowledge is meant to be had only by those who are privy to its power. This movie scene was a symbolic expression of this concept.

Ashram - The meeting place of the way to knowledge. The way of knowledge is one of the three ways of Hindu salvation. This salvation is not the same as that found in Christianity. It is the freedom from earthly attachments and the re-incarnation cycle. The other two means of escape are works (Karma Marga) and devotion (Bhakti Marga). The house where Jay and I met with other disciples to do kundalini yoga was called an ashram since those methods were meant to enlighten the individual with knowledge, although there was also the devotion aspect involved in many of the meditations. It comes from the more modern Hindu-based term 'Ashramas' which are the four stages for the ideal life of the Brahmin. Paramahansa Yogananda is one of the most recognizable names among western students of yoga. He wrote *Autobiography of a Yogi*, and helped start the SRF (Self-Realization Fellowship).

Chakra - An energy center within the body, usually associated with an organ or endocrine gland. For example, the lowest chakra at the root of the spine is associated with the sex organs. The highest is often associated with the pineal gland in the brain, though some schools say there is a highest chakra actually 'above' the body. When it is stimulated in an enlightened person, it gives the appearance of a halo. I found it interesting that different meditations in kundalini were intended to stimulate different chakras of the body, and in the AMO, we were taught that chanting different vowel sounds would stimulate various organs and glands for health and spiritual growth. This was obviously the same principle at work defined differently in eastern and western terminology.

Cosmic consciousness (Christ conscious-ness) - These two terms are closely related to one another, and to many are identical. They describe a state of higher spiritual enlightenment. To many western mystical philosophies, such as the Order, this is the goal of arcane instructions and esoteric practices. Yet, it is also more than a goal. It can also be seen as the spring-board to the next step in one's evolution. To many, achieving cosmic consciousness means an escape from the re-incarnation cycle, for all karmic debts have been paid, and all necessary knowledge to move on has been obtained. Obviously, Christ conscious-ness is a term derived from the Bible (*christos* is the Greek word for anointed, i.e., the Messiah). It is cosmic consciousness framed in more traditional western religious terminology. See also <u>nirvana</u>, as this is basically the same concept or goal described from a more eastern background and per-spective.

Divine Mother Force - See <u>Gaia</u> (or <u>Gaea</u>). One of several terms for the impersonal creative force behind the physical and spiritual evolution of the universe. The feminine aspect tends more toward the life-giving and nurturing aspects of The Force.

Esoteric - Regarding knowledge and teaching, it is instruction intended for a select few disciples. It is privileged information. One of the lures of the secret mystery schools and occult practices is the sense of being among the spiritual elite. See also <u>arcane</u>.

Gaia (or Gaea) - From Greek mythology, this is the earth goddess and mother of the Titans. In modern Aquarian thought, she symbolizes the concept of our planet as a living entity. We are all a part of this unified 'being' in a monistic reality. If we mix in the idea of evolution and spontaneous generation, that we have our origins in the primordial soup, then the elements of nature are our ancestors. This truly makes the earth our Mother. Mother Nature is Mother Earth is *our* Mother.

Karma - This term has its origin in Sanskrit, meaning deed. It relates to the law of cause and effect regarding spiritual matters. It is not necessarily justice as in an eye for an eye, though this is not disregarded. It is more along the lines of causes yielding effects that manifest in order to evolve each individual toward the goal of escaping the earthly re-incarnation cycle. Surprisingly, this aspect of karma is becoming more developed in the western world. Generally speaking, one sees more charity manifesting in the west, probably due to its historical basis in Christianity. This concept carries over into the westernized definition of karma. The master at our ashram referred to charity and good deeds as karma yoga, selfless works for the ultimate benefit of self.

Lost Word - The Order taught that various vowel and consonant sounds could impact reality and influence our spiritual growth. The most commonly known is probably OM, which, if chanted, is supposed to calm the mind, body, and soul. But more importantly, its repetition is intended to harmonize one with his environment and with the universe, which will in turn aid one's personal evolution to godhood. The lost word was another such sound combination. It was taught that it was somehow involved in the creation of our current physical universe. I always had difficulty understanding the significance of a personal being like myself deliberately chanting the lost word in order to understand how an impersonal force accidentally uttered this sound for the result of creating the universe; but, this was a result which was not designed, because it originated from an impersonal force incapable of designing. Do you see the problem I had with this?

Maya - Illusion of the physical world. It is more literally a term describing the Hindu concept that ultimate reality of this phenomenal world is to be denied. This term has its roots in the Upanishads, any of a group of ancient Vedic commentaries. These Vedas are any or all four of the ancient sacred writings of Hinduism. Veda in Sanskrit means knowledge. Thus, knowledge of this world reveals that it is illusory. This relates to the New Age concept of non-naturalism. This philosophy says that reality is neither naturalistic only, nor does it perceive the supernatural as something separate from the natural. There is no supernatural, because nothing in the spirit world transcends the physical world. They are in unity in a monistic causal reality. Actuality is non-naturalism, meaning that the natural, physical world is only a part of the total spiritual essence of all that is. As above, so below. The physical world is only a part of the totality of being. The problem with the concept of maya is that of circular logic. If knowledge of this world reveals it to be an illusion, then there is no way of knowing that such knowledge is real, and is not itself an illusion. Nothing can be accurately defined as meaningful. This starts moving us from mystical spiritualism to philosophical nihilism.

Nirvana - In Buddhism, this is the desired goal wherein one achieves a state of heavenly peace in that the soul becomes free of all desire and pain. It is paradoxical that this freedom from desire is what is desired. It is interesting that this Buddhist term has its origins in Sanskrit, the ancient language of India. That original meaning was extinction. This fits the idea of becoming one with the universe, if such oneness is viewed as becoming 'extinct' in the personal sense. This was one of the fearful experiences I had in kundalini and in spirit defense of karate, i.e., the loss of personal identity. It also correlates with one of the rational difficulties I had with the idea of evolving out of the personal into the impersonal. Such a notion makes man the lowest evolutionary form of life on earth, because he is the most personal. While we can argue that humans are earth's lowest life form in humorous satire, the irrationality of such a position is actually quite obvious.

Noosphere - A term from Pierre Teilhard de Chardin, a Jesuit paleontologist and philosopher. In my religion class, we studied his work, *The Phenomena of Man*, written in 1965. Noos is from the Greek word *nous*, meaning mind. Thus, noosphere is a single-word definition for the ultimate blending of all human consciousness into one planetary mind. A New Ager wants to evolve to a higher level of consciousness. This individual spiritual evolution will also manifest as a planetary evolution for the human race, in which each individual consciousness will be a neuron in the planetary mind, the noosphere. This associates with the concept of the individual becoming one with the universe. Thus, atonement means at-one-ment.

Paradigm Shift - The word paradigm has its origin in Greek, *paradeigma*, meaning pattern. The New Age paradigm shift refers to a cataclysmic change in the pattern of mankind's universe as he currently understands it. This may manifest only spiritually as mankind enters his next stage of evolution, but there may be some physical manifestations as well. In the fringe groups I briefly encountered in the mid-80's, New Agers saw radical changes on the horizon. These include changes in the fabric of society, the physical world, and mankind's universal state of spiritual awareness. The harmonic convergence of December 31, 1986 was intended to move the planet closer to this paradigm shift in evolution. One of the originators of this event considers Christians to be anti-Christ because they deny the divinity within each individual, and are thus holding back the planet's emergence into the new age of light, life, and love.

Spirit Defense - As Chin put this to me in karate, it was a method of becoming one with the creative force of the universe for the purpose of self-defense. If we allow our spiritual 'senses' to develop and attune to this force, amazing things can be accomplished in both yoga and the martial arts, because our bodies and minds are able to transcend the boundaries of the physical plane. Since the Divine Mother Force is life-loving, it (she?) is life-protecting. Therefore, these skills must not be used for selfish motives or abused to unduly injure one's adversary.

Theosophy - From the Greek *theos* (god) and *sophos* (wise), thus it literally means wise god or the wisdom of the gods. The Theosophical Society in the United States was started around 1875, although its headquarters were moved to India shortly after it began. Its aims were to unite mankind under the brotherhood of all religions, although it was mainly Hindu, with considerable Buddhist influence. The term theosophy was originally associated with the Society, although now it generally means any discipline or philosophical system which claims insight into personal divine nature through instruction and technique. Thus, my affiliation with the Order could be classified as an affiliation with theosophy. In fact, there were

268

many in the Order who thought there was a great deal of influence and even origin of the Order with the original Theosophist Society. However, the Order claimed its teachings went back to ancient Egypt and the mystery schools of the Far East. But so did the Theosophists.

Witchcraft - It is often called 'The Old Religion,' indicating its roots in pre-Christian antiquity. The old English term, *wicca*, means wisdom or knowledge. It is difficult to give a brief and general definition, because there are so many varied forms of sorcery, divination, magical arts, etc., with origins in virtually every historical culture. Most agree the recent resurgence in the west began with Alister Crowley (1875-1947). He enjoyed referring to himself as the Great Beast of Revelation. Anton La Vey, author of *The Satanic Bible*, founded the First Church of Satan in San Francisco. To him, Satan is a symbolic term representing the Force, which can be tapped for power and success. The practitioners of Wicca with whom I came in contact, were involved in "white magic," practiced for the benefit of others. They shared with me that there are more selfish witches whose primary purpose was self-gain, and if others got in the way of this mission, then so be it ("So mote it be"). It is possible to see philosophical associations between

269

witchcraft and movements based in the power of femininity, since there is a tradition of tapping the creative 'feminine side' of the Force in modern white witchcraft. The power of sex can play a part in some forms of the craft as well. Christians, witches, and Satanists all agree with one another that the power manifested in these practices is real. They disagree on the source of this power.

Wadena - Little round hill. Native American origin. Wadena House was the family residence while Dr. Phillips was at Oxford University in England. The house sat on a little round hill. It was located just east of the main spires of High Street in the region of Shotover Hill. In this part of Oxford, houses are named rather than designated by number and street. The first two books to be published by Wadena House Books were written by Dr. Phillips in his little office at Wadena House overlooking the horse field next door. Legend has it that when this spot was just a knoll in the terrain, it was a meeting place for royalty and nobles on the Old London Road between Oxford and Regent's Park in London.

Visit us at – www.wadenahousebooks.com!

Glossary